VIRGINIA
Off the Beaten Path

"The adventurous authors have found those unique attractions only seen when you step off the well-trod tourist path. They paint a picture of Virginia that perhaps you never knew existed."
— *AAA World*

"This is a Virginia connoisseur's guide. . . . It will tell you about places that you probably don't know about, even if you've traveled in Virginia before."
— *The Journal,* Montgomery County, MD

"Will take you to and through that historic state in style."
— *Rockland* (ME) *Courier-Gazette*

"A wealth of unusual excursions. From factories to farms to fabulous restaurants, the Colberts cover it all and then some."
— *Mid-Atlantic Country*

"Covers from the hill country in the southwest corner, through the Shenandoah valley to the Tidewater area of the northeast. It features easy-to-follow directions, hours, and price ranges along with maps and photographs."
— *The Star,* Chicago, IL

"A good companion guide for a traveler. . . . [with] lots of interesting tidbits that make a trip a little more special."
— *Winchester* (MA) *Star*

VIRGINIA
Off the Beaten Path
Second Edition

by **Judy and Ed Colbert**

A Voyager Book

Chester, Connecticut

Library of Congress Cataloging-in-Publication Data

Colbert, Judy.
  Virginia : off the beaten path / by Judy and Ed Colbert : photos and maps by the authors. — 2nd ed.
      p.   cm.
    "A Voyager book."
    Includes index.
    ISBN 0-87106-624-6
    1. Virginia — Description and travel—1981- —Guide-books.
  I. Colbert, Ed.   II. Title.
  F224.3.C65   1989   89—7565
  917.5504 '43—dc20   CIP

Manufactured in the United States of America
Second Edition/First Printing

To
Harry and Bernice Mudrick and
Arthur and Frederica Colbert,
who started us on our way.

Contents

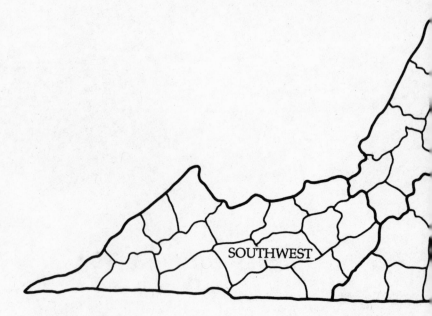

SOUTHWEST

Virginia

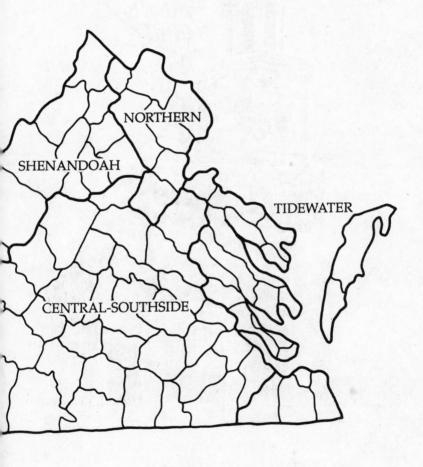

NORTHERN

SHENANDOAH

TIDEWATER

CENTRAL-SOUTHSIDE

Christ Church, Alexandria

Introduction

Touring the Commonwealth of Virginia takes a special frame of mind, for it is a very special state of marvelous contradictions and fantastic opportunities. On the eastern shore and in Tidewater, the geography offers seaside and waterfront where you can drown yourself in the pleasures of the water and some of the best seafood in the world. In the Shenandoah and southwest highlands, you are treated to rugged mountains of breathtaking beauty. We call these mountains friendly mountains, for they invite you to walk through them (unlike the Rockies, which are spectacular to look at but not so easy to explore). Populations vary from towns of under a hundred to cities of half a million. Virginia is steeped in historical importance and, although very much into today's world, Virginians spend a great deal of time and effort in remembering.

As we've toured Virginia over the years, we've always paid special interest to places and people who don't receive a great deal of attention. That's why a large portion of this book is spent away from the arranged attractions of King's Dominion, Busch Gardens, and Colonial Williamsburg. Even the magnificent Skyline Drive and Blue Ridge Parkway are barely mentioned. That doesn't mean they don't have delicious secrets of their own; it just means we haven't concentrated on them in this book. Of course, big cities keep secrets as well, so we've tried to give some of them their due exploration time.

When you approach a state as diverse and large as Virginia for a book such as *Virginia: Off the Beaten Path,* however, it's inevitable that something will be omitted. There just wasn't space for everything we wanted to include or that might have been included. We look to you for suggestions for the next revision, and we hope you will share your special treasures with us.

We have listed prices for some items (admissions, meals) and operating times; these should be taken as guidelines, not ironclad guarantees. Many places have been open only seasonally but are changing to year-round operation. When the Blue Ridge Parkway is closed to cars because of snow, that means it might be open to cross-country skiers. If you're going to drive a long distance to see something, call first to obtain the most current information.

Because so many of the places are not on the many interstates that crisscross Virginia, we recommend a good Virginia map.

Introduction

When you stop at any of the Virginia welcome stations, they will give one to you without charge.

Another interesting and useful free companion sightseeing publication is the "Virginia Travel Guide for the Disabled," published by the Opening Door, Inc., a nonprofit charity devoted to encouraging the disabled to travel through Virginia. The 96 pages are filled with listings of hotels, motels, restaurants, and tourist attractions, with comments about their accessibility (bathroom, walkways, doorways, telephones, and special guides). It is available at the Virginia tourist centers or by writing to the Opening Door, Inc., Route 2, Box 1805, Woodford 22580.

This is the twentieth anniversary of what is arguably the most enduring little sentence of the past two decades. As the Virginia Division of Tourism states, "It is not of great political import; it does not stir the soul. It is, of all things, a bumper-sticker slogan: 'Virginia is for lovers.' It has become a much-imitated part of the national language." And it all started in Virginia, the Old Dominion.

For a booklet about Virginia tourism, call (800) 248–4833 or write to the Division of Tourism at 202 North Ninth Street, Suite 500, Richmond 23219. The Division of Tourism (804–786–4484) can also provide more specific information about an area. We could not have found so many wonderful people and places if it had not been for their help. We particularly thank Martha Steger, a very special person in a very special state—Virginia.

We hope you enjoy reading and exploring *Virginia: Off the Beaten Path* as much as we enjoyed researching and writing it.

Off the Beaten Path in Southwest Virginia

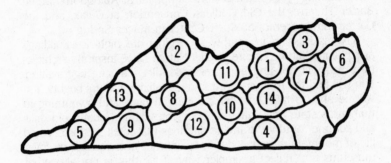

1. Bland County
   Big Walker Lookout
2. Buchanan County
   Breaks Interstate Park
3. Giles County
   covered bridges
   Mountain Lake Hotel
   Jefferson National Forest
4. Grayson County
   Nautilus, Inc.
   Rooftop of Virginia Craft
     Center
   Jeff Matthews Memorial
     Museum
5. Lee County
   Cumberland Gap
6. Montgomery County
   Christiansburg Depot
   The Farmhouse
   Jacob's Lantern
7. Pulaski County
   Carousel Village
   Wilderness Road Regional
     Museum
8. Russell County
   Russell County Courthouse
9. Scott County
   Natural Tunnel

10. Smyth County
    Saltville Fitness Trail
    Carter Family Fold
11. Tazewell County
    Historic Crab Orchard
      Museum and
      Pioneer Park
    Burkes Garden
    Pocahontas Exhibition
      Coal Mine
12. Washington County
    Barter Theatre
    Virginia Creeper Trail
    Country Gourmet
    Tri-State Livestock Market
    White's Mill
    Kern's Bakery
13. Wise County
    Coal Museum
    June Tolliver House
    Southwest Virginia
      Museum
14. Wythe County
    Rural Retreat
    Blue Ridge Books
    Wytheville State Fish
      Hatchery
    shot tower

Southwest Virginia

Southwest Virginia reflects the pioneer spirit that made its way across this, America's first frontier. And just because the hills are known for their stills, don't take backwoods to be backwards. Internationally renowned celebrities appear at Abingdon's famed Barter Theatre, the Old Fiddlers' Convention at Galax, and the Carter Family Memorial Music Center in Maces Spring.

What is missing in southwest Virginia are high-rise buildings and polluted air to obscure Mother Nature's awe-inspiring architecture. You will not find high-pressured, ulcer-causing aggravation. You will find the frontier spririt and revitalizing natural beauty. You will be able to take time for camping, fishing, and swimming in numerous state and national parks. You will find quaint old mills and summer outdoor dramatic offerings that retell the history and life of mountain days decades and centuries ago. You will discover museums that reflect a simpler way of life that is not altogether absent from today's way of going about things.

In our first edition of *Virginia: Off the Beaten Path* we said, "It's a safe bet that tourism will never be a number one industry in any of these counties, for the roads couldn't handle the traffic." That is still true, except that plans are being discussed on ways to increase tourism in West Virginia, bringing more people from Virginia into that state. Any railroad or scenic parkway that takes traffic that way can bring traffic this way. Other economic boosts are being made to this area, which has been so dependent upon coal, including new shopping centers, a Buster Brown children's clothing factory, and the state's new $32 million prison. All of this creates an infrastructure that can only help the residents and visitors.

To those of us who love these hills and the quiet ways, the lack of tourism is a shame and a blessing: a shame for there is a great deal to see, do, and share and a blessing because it means there are not thousands of tourists crowding the area. Economic reality, however, says southwest Virginia has so much to offer and teach others that it should be an opportunity enjoyed by all.

Bland County

James A. Williams, editor and publisher of the *Southwest Virginia Enterprise* newspaper and chairman of the Great Lakes to

Florida Association, fought hard to have Interstate 77 routed along its current path. The dual-lane divided ribbon of road comes down West Virginia through the twin towns of Bluefield (the highest elevation city of its size in the country), through Bland County, and past Wytheville where it joins up with Interstate 81 for a while. The *Enterprise* is published in Wytheville.

This span of Interstate 77, which includes two tunnels, one through East River Mountain and the other through Big Walker Mountain, parallels what Williams described as the "notorious" Route 21. Each tunnel is about a mile long and saves the traveler from 10 to 20 miles of serpentine and hilly roadway.

You experience some of this torture (of the pleasurable kind) when you travel off Interstate 77 along Route 21 to the **Big Walker Lookout** (703-228-4401). The Appalachian Trail goes through this area, affording many vistas. There also is a commercial overlook with a tourist shop, a swinging bridge to a chair lift (the first and tallest in Virginia), a snake pit, and other "attractions." Of course, the main attraction is the view. In spring it's highlighted by the newborn blossoms; in fall, by the flaming foliage.

The chair lift is open daily during the summer and weekends only in the spring and fall. There is an admission charge to Big Walker Lookout. From Bland and Interstate 77, take the Bland exit south onto Routes 21 and 52 for 8 miles. From Wytheville and Interstate 81, take exit 21 north for 12 miles on Routes 21 and 52.

Buchanan County

Buchanan County has seen all four types of mining operations—auger, deep, strip, and truck—and the county is noted for leading all Virginia counties in coal production.

Breaks Interstate Park in Buchanan (the first syllable is pronounced "buck") County boasts an area called the "Grand Canyon of the South." In an area of 2,670 acres, the Russell Fork of the Big Sandy River has carved a deep gorge through the sandstones of Pine Mountain. The river goes over and around huge boulders in waterfalls and rapids and drops about 450 feet in 5 miles through the Breaks. Stop by the Museum/Information Center for interpretative displays and audiovisual aids for the natural and historical features of the area, a coal exhibit describing the primary industry in the surrounding areas, and information on such things as the Hatfield-McCoy feud. Travel Highway 460 from Grundy to Harman Junction, then Route 609 to the Breaks.

Giles County

Two of the seven **covered bridges** remaining in Virginia are located in Giles County, near Newport. They are modified William Howe bridges (in 1840 he combined iron uprights with wooden supports, creating the forerunner of the steel bridge) and cross Sinking Creek. A 55-foot bridge used to be along the Appalachian Trail near Route 700 (Mountain Lake Road) but was bypassed by a realignment of the trail. The bridge was left in place so the property owner could use it when a new bridge was built in 1949. The second, a 70-foot span, was left in place when a new bridge was constructed in 1963. More offensive than the deterioration of what appears to be a 1912 bridge (the state says circa 1916) is the four-letter-word graffiti that prohibits our publishing a picture of the bridge.

Farther up Route 700 in Pembroke is the **Mountain Lake Hotel,** an old resort that has been catering to summer visitors for years. Although former manager Joseph "Mac" McMillin says people still tell him they or their relatives stood on the fire line fighting the blaze that destroyed the old (1850s) wooden structure, in fact it was torn down and rebuilt in 1936 with stone cut from the property.

Even if you have never visited Mountain Lake, you may feel you know the place, for it was featured in the movie *Dirty Dancing* with Patrick Swayze and Jennifer Grey.

Mountain Lake has only recently begun staying open through the winter season. After a multi-million–dollar renovation that includes Jacuzzi tubs in some rooms and a new lodge building in addition to the old lodge, H.M. "Buzz" Scanlan, marketing director, says the response has been terrific, and they plan to continue to keep it open as a year-round resort with an off-season emphasis on conferences and thematic outings devoted to computer training, finances, wine tastings, the current murder mystery fad, and the like.

The dining room offers gracious service, a pleasant house wine, and fairly good food (the duckling with kumquats, cherries, and grapes is superb). Of course, after a day of fresh air and exercise, anything is likely to taste good, but this is delightful. About twenty-five non-hotel guests can be seated in the dining room, but reservations are essential.

Mountain Lake is the highest lake in Virginia (4,000 feet elevation), one of only two natural lakes, and the highest inhabited mountain in the state.

Activities abound, including fishing in the 250-acre Mountain Lake (the chef will cook your catch of the day, which might be a largemouth bass, a rainbow or palomino trout, or even a four-inch bream), tennis, and golf in the summer (the nine-hole golf course is due to be changed to a two-tee eighteen-hole course). And, there are ice skating and cross-country skiing (rentals available) in the winter. "Dirty Dancing" lessons are offered periodically, so you can make believe you are Baby or Johnny Castle. Photography is marvelous all year, with wild azaleas and rhododendrons in the spring, blazing leaves in the fall, and crystal snow scenes from January and through March.

Lodging starts at about $100 a night and includes three meals a day and activities. Unless you buy sundries while you're there, you don't need to take out your wallet. Call (703) 626-7121 or (800) 346-3334.

Jefferson National Forest blankets large sections of several counties, and an entire book could be compiled on the various trails and activities within the system. As a sampling we'll use the part of the forest in the area around Giles County that is supervised from the Blacksburg ranger station. A visit to the Blacksburg office will find Ranger George G. Marlin, Virginia Powell, and W. Alan Guthrie eager to help you with all your questions and suggest things you'll enjoy doing.

Among the activities is a 2-mile hike to view the **Cascades,** a spectacular 60-foot waterfall. Approach is via Little Stony Creek (stocked with trout), past a steam boiler from an old sawmill (1918–1922) and an awesome look at Barney's Wall (a sheer bluff rising from the creek bed to a height of 3,640 feet) from the bottom of the bluff. The hike along this easy-to-moderately difficult trail should take three and a half hours.

Up from Mountain Lake is **Minie (or Minnie) Ball Hill,** a great place to find Civil War souvenirs. According to legend, General George Crook, pressed by Confederate troops and bogged down by muddy trails, was forced to abandon an extra weight of ammunition and perhaps even a cannon full of gold (some say it's at the bottom of Mountain Lake). Lead bullets or "minie balls" left behind on May 12, 1864, are still found by those who search the area.

Actually, minie balls do not refer to size, but to French Army Captain Claude Etienne Minie who developed the bullet-shaped projectile that could be shot from a muzzle loading rifle.

Take a hike along **Sinking Creek Mountain,** named for a streambed that tends to dry up in the summer months, or go up to **Hanging Rock** for a 360-degree look at the world. An old fire tower is good for watching the spring (April) and fall (mid-September to mid-October) migrations of redtail, broadwing and sharpshinned hawks. Call Jim Frazier at Virginia Polytechnic Institute and State University, also known as Virginia Tech or VPI, (703-961-6064) for more precise dates.

Audie Murphy, the most decorated United States soldier from World War II, died in an airplane crash on May 28, 1971 on Brush Mountain. The Veterans of Foreign Wars has placed a monument to him on the crash site, which you can visit.

A Sportsman's Map of Jefferson National Forest is available from the ranger station for $1. It shows the old route of the Appalachian Trail, so be sure to mark in the new way before you set out on your travels.

Grayson County

If you assume all manufacturing plants are now a mass of robots, you should visit **Nautilus, Inc.,** a manufacturer of exercise equipment, including a line of handicapped-accessible pieces, the first in the industry. Not only is there not a robot on the premises, but all equipment is made to order, so there is not a bunch of gear sitting around waiting to be sold.

Margaret Stuart, director of personnel, will take special civic groups and student classes through the plant to see how the production of gym and health club equipment progresses from assembly to painting to upholstery. Advance tour reservations are requested; call (703) 773-2881.

Located in Independence, just east of the intersection of Routes 21 and 58 and 221 on Powerhouse Road.

The **Rooftop of Virginia Craft Center,** housed in a cathedral-type setting, is part of Rooftop of Virginia CAP, a community action agency that hosts senior citizen activities as well as Head Start programs. Located in Galax, work is done by native craftspeople; the center offers for sale such authentic handmade items as pottery, wood carvings, quilts, and needlework. If you're stopping at either the Grayson Highlands State Park or the Mount Rogers National Recreation Area during the summer, you'll find some of these crafts available as well. The center is open 9:00 A.M. to 5:00 P.M. Monday through Saturday during the summer, and 9:00 A.M. to 4:30 P.M. Tuesday through Saturday in January, February, and March. It is at 206 North Main Street; call (703) 236-7131.

Jeff Matthews Memorial Museum is housed in two pioneer cabins (one constructed in 1834). Thousands of Indian and mountaineer artifacts, as well as items from outside the area, are on display. This is a fascinating collection of 8,500 items in five dozen cases put together by Jeff Matthews, his family, and citizens of Galax and the surrounding area; it takes about an hour to view.

Among the things you'll see are over 1,000 different knives collected by Matthews, newspapers dating back to January 4, 1800, covering George Washington's burial, and 40 mounted heads and animal rugs from other parts of the country collected by Glenn Pless.

"New" additions to the museum, according to curator Rita Edwards, include a collection of old dental equipment from local dentist Dr. Paul Katt, who was still practicing dentistry in 1988 when he died, in his eighties. Among the equipment are his chair, an X-ray machine, and tools of his trade from an earlier generation. Work still is progressing on the Confederate soldier display, with two rooms showing pictures of all the men they could locate from Galax, Grayson, and other nearby towns who fought in the Confederate War.

The museum is open Wednesday, Thursday, and Friday from 1:00 P.M. to 5:00 P.M., Saturday from 11:00 A.M. to 4:00 P.M., and Sunday from 1:00 P.M. to 4:00 P.M. It's closed on Monday and Tuesday. The visit is free, but donations are accepted. It is located adjacent to the Vaughan Memorial Library at 606 West Stuart Drive in Galax; call (703) 236-7874.

Other events in the area are the Whitetop Mountain Maple Festival in March at the Mt. Rogers Fire Hall (703-388-3283); the Truck and Tractor Pull at Felts Park, Galax in early May (703-236-

2772); the Whitetop Mountain Ramp Festival in mid-May at the Mt. Rogers Fire Hall (703–388–3283); the Labor Day Gun Show & Flea Market (proclaimed the best show in the South—a sellout) over Labor Day weekend (703–728–2035); and the Mountain Foliage Festival with music, crafts, food, and a band competition in mid-October (P.O. Box 315, Independence 24348). The annual Grand Privy Race, where people raced privies on wheels down Main Street, Independence, has been cancelled recently. There was no lack of competitors, but a lack of organizational workers. If enough interest is expressed in resuming this event, it should be rescheduled.

Lee County

Lee County, the most southwestern of Virginia's counties, comes to a point with the state borders of Kentucky and Tennessee at **Cumberland Gap.** Getting there along Route 58 is an experience that can just about make you forget there's a highly industrialized civilization just a few miles away. Once you leave Duffield (Scott County), it's a pleasant drive along a two-lane mountainous road of about 50 miles, past serene, checkerboarded pastures, little towns, white churches of assorted denominations, vent-sided barns filled with drying burley tobacco, closed-sided barns for livestock, wildflowers, large satellite antenna dishes, and cemeteries.

Historical markers periodically line the road, relating the comings and goings of Indians, such as the June 1785 massacre by a notorious half-breed known as Benge. Two miles west of Rose Hill is an Indian burial mound, most likely Cherokee.

Once you reach the Gap, you have to go into Kentucky to reach the visitors center, where there are displays on the Civil War and about Daniel Boone and the thirty axemen who cut the Wilderness Trail in 1775. Some 300,000 pioneers came through this pass in the following twenty-five years. The Wilderness Trail wasn't "off the beaten path" then. It *was* the path. It's not so crowded these days.

The Pinnacle, reached via a 4-mile drive from the visitors center, overlooks the three states and the Gap. The drive is off limits to trailers and vehicles over 20 feet long. Along with Route 58, these roads can give new meaning to the term *hairpin turn.*

Leaves start turning in this neck of the woods as early as 125 days before Christmas, but the peak is later in the fall. During the fall you're likely to find the view fogged much of the time, but you can buy slides of what the view would look like at the visitors center.

Camping (160 sites—no utility hookups, but there is a dump station), nature hikes, hot showers, campfire programs at the amphitheater, and other activities are available, but most of them are scheduled during the summer (Memorial Day through Labor Day). A limited number of backcountry permits are issued. Call (606) 248–2817.

Construction has started on a new 1-mile tunnel that will eliminate the need to drive over the last mountain before reaching the Kentucky town of Middlesboro, but it may be 1993 to 1995 before it's completed.

Montgomery County

The basically unheralded work of Jim and Helen Dorsett can be found in the old town section of Cambria, where they publish the quarterly *Scale Cabinetmaker* and make furniture miniatures. The Dorsetts are also working to restore the 1868 **Christiansburg Depot,** a railroad freight station that replaced the previous station burned in 1864 by Union soldiers. Jim says it's the "only architecturally complete depot built after the Civil War that is left" on the Virginia and Tennessee lines. The Victorian Italianate design, with its tower, gables, and eaves, was doomed to demolition until the Dorsetts bought it and started the restoration. On April 16, 1985, the depot was placed on the Virginia Landmarks Registry.

The Dorsetts are doing this for those of you who've never seen an old station with its "Ladies Waiting Room" (husbands were allowed in the ladies' side, but women weren't allowed in the men's side). Even if you've seen such a facility, stop by and talk to the Dorsetts. They'll walk you around the building, showing pictures of the project and explaining how they figured the bottom 25 inches of the building had been cut off at one point because of rotten timbers. There's no admission fee, but they'll gladly accept donations. The depot is on Cambria at the railroad tracks.

The Dorsetts also have purchased the building across the street and have started restoration work on that. Call (703) 382–4651 for information.

For additional information about the Cambria-Christiansburg area, call Kathy Mantz, who heads the local Chamber of Commerce, at (703) 382–4251.

In the center of Christiansburg, the county seat, at 2 East Main Street, is a 1936 post office with a WPA mural by John DeGroot entitled *Great Road*. This 1939 Mural American Art painting is one of about two dozen post office murals and sculptures created in Virginia through the Works Projects Administration. Painted and sculpted in the late 1930s and early 1940s, they were part of one of the programs Roosevelt's New Deal administration funded to keep unemployed artists working.

Christiansburg's Main Street was part of Daniel Boone's Wilderness Trail, mentioned earlier in this section under Lee County. Another historical event took place here when in May 1808 Thomas Lewis and John McHenry were involved in the first duel with rifles known to have taken place in Virginia. Both men died. This duel led to the passage of the Barbour Bill in January 1810, which outlawed dueling in Virginia. Dr. John Floyd was the attending physician and later went on to be governor of Virginia and a member of Congress. A marker in Christiansburg at Routes 11 and 460 designates the spot.

The continental divide in the western part of the country marks the ridge where all rainwater falling to the west of the divide flows into the Pacific and that falling to the east makes its way to the Atlantic. There are other "continental" divides, and the Eastern Continental Divide runs through the Christiansburg and Blacksburg areas. All the water to the east of this divide flows through the Roanoke River into the Atlantic. The water to the west runs into the New River and eventually to the Ohio and Mississippi rivers and on to the Gulf of Mexico before spilling into the Atlantic. Unfortunately, there are no signs indicating the location of this ridge. Look instead for where the New River has etched through limestone, leaving spectacular towering formations hundreds of feet tall.

Dinner at David Linewand's **The Farmhouse** is a singular treat. You'll find a building that is over 100 years old, with the restaurant occupying the place since 1962. Restaurant manager Barbara Wade started here as a waitress when it opened and can take you on a delightful tour through the original building and its additions. Decorations include wooden paneling, antiques, and art works such as a carousel shield from an 1895 New York ride that was dismantled when LaGuardia Airport was built. The shield, with its oil painting of John Adams, was one of a set depicting the first eighteen presidents. You'll find Cream of Wheat advertisements and drawings in the main ladies' room, an old wooden Indian, and Virginia Tech yearbooks dating back to the 1950s and 1960s.

The menu is on your paper placemat with dinners and the prime rib is extraordinary, and a piece ordered rare comes out rare, but warm. Dinner is enjoyed to the strains of classical music. The desserts include black and white cheesecake, grasshopper cake, midnight layer cake, lemon chess and chocolate chess pie, and chocolate luscious pie. You probably won't go wrong with any dessert choice, but the lemon chess and the grasshopper have particularly personalized endorsements.

The Farmhouse (703–382–4253) is open from 5:00 P.M. to 11:00 P.M. Monday through Saturday, and from noon to 9:00 P.M. on Sunday. It's on Cambria Street, just at the outer limits of Christiansburg.

When you travel through Blacksburg you may hear the legend of **Jacob's Lantern.** It's a tale about Jacob Harbrook, who lived in a cabin on the west bank of the northerly flowing waters of the New River. One version says he lived before the French and Indian War of the mid-1750s. His wife had been killed years earlier by Indians, so with his lantern he scouted the high cliffs along the swift-moving river to guide the pioneers safely across and through territory often bothered by marauding Indians. He saved many lives by preventing surprise Indian attacks. He was supposedly killed in 1755 by Indians when he tried to save hostages taken in the massacre at Draper's Meadow. Another version says Jacob stood guard over the river and railroad, using his lantern to announce safe passage for trains, arms shipments, and personnel. This tale, however, is set during the Civil War, more than 100 years later than the first tale.

Both legends continue on to say that his lantern light still can be seen during a full moon, reflecting off the waters of the New River, signalling that Jacob's spirit continues its patrol. And so, the restaurant at the Blacksburg Marriott bears the name Jacob's Lantern. Whichever tale you hear, remember it's just a legend created by previous Marriott management to go along with the name of their restaurant. Some people say some people will believe anything.

Regardless of what you believe, you should believe in Jacob's Lantern's caramel ice cream pie (graham cracker crust with coffee and vanilla ice cream, topped with caramel sauce and whipped cream) and the mud pie (Oreo cookie crust with brandy and Kahlua, chocolate ice cream, and fudge topping), each $2.25 and both created by pastry chef Cornelia "Neilly" Smith. Neilly has "retired" these days, but still come back on a part-time basis. The Marriott is at 900 Prices Ford Road. Call (703) 552–7001.

Pulaski County

A mile or less off Interstate 81 and away from the rush of today's traffic is a town from yesterday. The entire 1-mile-long linear town of Newbern, basically located on the Olde Wilderness Road, was declared a historic district in 1979. The land was granted to early settlers by King George III in 1772. At an altitude of 2,135 feet, the town, with its beautiful sunsets and surrounding mountains, reminded the settlers of Bern, Switzerland.

Annis F. Farris has been postmaster since 1968, overseeing ninety-five mailboxes and the day's business of Newbern. But in January 1988 a new post office was dedicated, the first ever built in Newbern for the specific purpose of being a post office. It has considerably more than ninety-five mailboxes and is located next to P.J.'s **Carousel Village.** Pat Hennon's craft shop, which used to be next to the post office, also has relocated to Carousel Village. Her former store is now the home of Buddy Fisher's Antique shop.

Within the Carousel Village are the carousel factory, antiques, ice cream, a gift shop, and the museum. Local crafts, including stuffed dolls, handmade quilts, and other decorative items are sold. The Christmas Shop is open all year with local and imported ornaments, nutcrackers, and lights. A 1923 carousel from the Cincinnati Zoo is open for rides. The Carousel Factory offers tours from 9:00 A.M. to 4:00 P.M. Monday through Friday, with prior notice. The carousel animals are created by P. J. Hennon or by one of P. J.'s artists. Jim Hennon's company makes these animals (a wood and polyester mixture) in several sizes from a tabletop model for about $47.50 to a working carousel for about $650.00

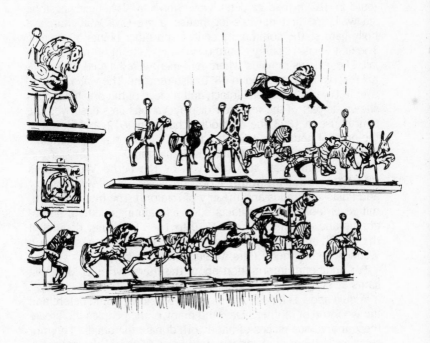

PJ's Carousel Collection

to full-size carnival and theme park creatures. Among the menagerie animals available are unicorn, goat, rabbit, rooster, polar bear, camel, tiger, lion, zebra, and giraffe. A catalog is available by writing to them at P.O. Box 355, Newbern, 24126, or by calling (703) 674–4300. Village hours are 10:00 A.M. to 6:00 P.M. Monday through Thursday, 10:00 A.M. to 9:00 P.M. Friday and Saturday, and 1:00 P.M. to 6:00 P.M. on Sunday. Call (703) 674–1249 for further information.

Daisy Williams is the town historian and leads walking tours of Newbern's historic spots, which include the Olde Newberne Jail (built in 1839), rose gardens, waterworks, a slave-built flagstone sidewalk, the first mayor's log house, a pre–Civil War church, a holly garden, the community center, and other points of interest. The first Pulaski County Courthouse stood in front of the Newbern jail. The gallows remains where two men were hanged. The original reservoir, constructed in 1870, also remains. The water system, over 100 years old, is still intact, and a piece of the original pipe is shown as part of the reservoir display. Various fires destroyed the courthouse in 1893, the Methodist church in 1912, and eleven of the original houses in 1924, but fifty-six of the original landmarks constructed between 1810 and 1895 still stand.

Mrs. Williams can also take you by Newbern's **Wilderness Road Regional Museum** (covering Floyd, Giles, Montgomery, and Pulaski counties and the city of Radford). The museum committee is looking for artifacts such as paintings, letters, photographs and documents from 1810 to 1865 to further document the growth and development of the area. The museum is open on Wednesday afternoon (Mrs. Williams has the key).

For additional information about the tours, write to Mrs. Williams at P.O. Box 373, Newbern 24216 or call (703) 674–5888.

A quilt show is held at the museum on the weekend before and the weekend of Mother's Day, and many of the people who create these marvelous pieces of handwork donate the quilts. The museum sells them, with prices starting at $50, and the proceeds benefiting the museum.

A walking tour brochure about Pulaski County (listing accomodations, restaurants, campgrounds, entertainment, a calendar of events, maps, tours, and attractions) is now available from the Pulaski County Chamber of Commerce, P.O. Box 169, Pulaski 24301, (703) 980–1991.

In 1965 Ruritan National, called the only rural American civic organization, opened its headquarters here. According to Curtis

Graham, coordinator of expansion development of new clubs, Ruritan organized in rural Holland, Virginia, in 1928, and for many years never had a national office. Directors wanted a place in Virginia, relatively near an interstate highway and an airport, but in a semirural area. With access to Interstates 77 and 81, the local club in nearby Dublin submitted a proposal for land donated by Burlington Industries, and so the Ruritans made this area their home. You're invited to visit daily between 8:30 A.M. and 5:00 P.M.; (703) 674–5431.

Russell County

A relatively new museum is in the works with the restoration of the old **Russell County Courthouse** at Dickensonville on Copper Creek, the first landmark in Russell County to be nominated to the National Register of Historic Places. The courthouse was used from late 1799 to 1818, when a new county seat was designated. Much work has been done on the exterior renovation and restoration, and now work is needed on the interior before it can be established as an artifacts museum, a place that students, residents, and tourists will find interesting enough to make it a major tourist attraction. For those wishing to assist in this project, write to E.S. "Bert" Fugate, Jr., Box 62, Lebanon 24210.

To see the courthouse, take Route 58/19 out of Abingdon to the Hansonville split and follow Route 58 to the left about 4 miles to Dickensonville.

Scott County

Natural Tunnel, an 850-foot-long tunnel that's as high as a ten-story building, was carved through the limestone rock of Powell's Mountain by Stock Creek's persistence. It's large enough for trains to go through, as well as people and the creek. An extensive work project has been going on here in the past few years that has created a new visitor center on top of the mountain. A new chair lift takes visitors down to the tunnel and is handicapped accessible. A fee will be charged. The exhibits, including the historical railroad museum, have not been installed into the new center yet, which will emphasize the natural history of the area more than the railroading impact.

17

Parking is $1.50, with a $1 pet charge in the picnicking area. Swimming is $1.75 for adults and $1.25 for children under 12. It is half price on weekdays after 3:00 P.M., but not on holidays or weekends. Camping season is April through November. The visitors center is open from 10:00 A.M. to 6:00 P.M. Memorial Day through Labor Day. Admission to the park area: Adults, $1; children ages 6 to 12, 75¢. From Clinchport, go north about two miles on U.S. 23, then a half mile east on Route 871. Call (703) 940–2674 for more information.

Nashville, Tennessee, may claim to be the home of country music, but the **Carter Family Fold** claims that A. P. Carter, his wife Sara, and her cousin Maybelle (mother of June, Helen, and Anita Carter) were the pioneers of this music form. The Carter Family recorded 300 songs between 1927 and 1942, 100 of them written by A. P. Now the Carter Family museum, Memorial Music Center, and Music in the Fold on Saturday nights at 7:30 show what country music, clogging, and buck dancing are about in a rustic country setting. An annual festival is held in August.

You'll find the Carter Family Fold in Maces Spring, just past Hiltons (Route 614, 3 miles east of Weber City). Call (703) 386–9480.

Smyth County

Just as your back (or whatever) is about to give out from hours of driving and riding while you're exploring the backroads and beautiful mountain scenery, along comes Saltville, the Salt Capital of the Confederacy. Suddenly, out of what appears to be almost nowhere, is the **Saltville Fitness Trail** running along the railroad tracks to help you work on your tired muscles and brain cells.

The first salt mine in America opened here in 1795. Apparently it wasn't really a mining operation, as the salt was removed from the ground in liquid form. The mine has been out of serious operation for some time, but the town is talking about pulling out enough salt to take care of its roads during the winter.

To become more intimately acquainted with the town, call Robert O. "Rocky" Cahill, chairman of the historical committee, at (703) 496–7377 for a historic tour. Or call the town hall at (703)

496–5342 for an informative booklet on the town's historic attractions. A museum contains Civil War history, information about the two Olin Chemical plants that used to be in Saltville, old salt kettles, and some of the wooden pipe that used to handle the saline solution.

Tazewell County

The **Historic Crab Orchard Museum and Pioneer Park** displays photos, multimedia presentations, and artifacts dating from millions of years ago to the present in a 110-acre area near Tazewell (it's a short *a*) designated as a prehistoric and historical archaeological area. Among the regular exhibits are a leg bone and teeth of a huge mastodon that roamed the area millions of years ago, the double palisades (protective fortification wall of tree trunks) of the native American, and relics from the Revolutionary and Civil wars.

A "Lepidodendron tree," which is really sandstone rock, might be the first thing you see as you enter the museum. The Lepidodendron was a popular growth item about 300,000,000 years ago and grew in the water that then covered the area. Eventually the trunk would break off and water would rot the interior, which would then fill with sand and form a cast of the inside of the tree trunk. Some of the wood would adhere to the stone, carbonize, and form bituminous coal.

The next thing you'll notice are the first of thirty-nine fashion dolls, dressed in clothing styles from 1790 to 1930 by Pete Ballard from Winston-Salem, North Carolina, who's very knowledgeable in textiles. A grant from the Hanes Foundation bought traveling cases for the dolls, so they can go on tour. You can also see what's left (the fur and skin) of "Old Hitler," a black bear who lived on nearby sheep. On the grounds are eight log structures showing the variety of notching styles used by the Scotch-Irish, German, and English, and two stone buildings.

Nellie Bundy is the director of this museum. She has always loved archaeology and used to dig in the area. After a notable career teaching history, she decided there should be a museum to show what had been found and what was known about southwest Virginia history. She is a wealth of information. She talks about retirement, but she has several projects she hasn't started or completed yet, so she may well be around for a few years.

As an example, in just a few years she has opened some of the cabins that were on the property; added three new buildings and an interpreters' cabin; developed a new horse-drawn–equipment exhibit and a new set of sheds to exhibit it; and staged a whole series of festivals and events, such as Halloween (complete with ghosts), fall classes, and Christmas singing. Another new display features fifteen native birds (stuffed) that are on the endangered species list.

Nellie has begun a perpetual dig on land across from the museum. They have done some excavation and uncovered a particular type of small doll, of which only one other has been found in Virginia, and it is now on display in the museum. This sixteen-acre section of land is on the National and State Historic and Prehistoric records. A particular section, dating back to 1550–1600, gives evidence of a long house. "What we have over there in the ground," says Nellie, "is very unusual for even the eastern part of the United States. It's a type of long house that is about 30 feet wide by 60 feet long, giving a rough figure, but it was outside of the palisades area and probably was used as a meeting house or something like that." She doesn't anticipate pulling up any skeletons but hopes rather to designate what areas were used for a storage bin, a fireplace, and so on.

The gift and craft shop on the premises has been enlarged and upgraded. Admission to the museum is $2 for adults, $1.50 for seniors, $1 for children ages four through twelve, and free for children under four. Group discounts are available if arrangements are made at least three weeks in advance. The museum is located 3 miles west of Tazewell on Routes 19 and 460 (the four-lane highway, not the business route); it is closed on Monday from April through October, and Sunday and Monday from November through March. Call (703) 988–6755 for further details.

The bed and breakfast is just coming to southwest Virginia with the opening of Betty VanDyke's home. This bed and breakfast comes complete with log cabin, the opportunity to chop your own wood if you wish, and a gorgeous view from downtown Tazewell. You can have coffee and buns in the morning or join Betty VanDyke for a full breakfast. Call (703) 988–4111. This is the number for her television sales and repair store, but she is there about half the time, so it is a good number to call.

Not too far from Tazewell is **Burkes Garden,** which was surveyed in 1748 and is now designated a Virginia Scenic Byway. This beautiful valley is unique because it is surrounded by only one mountain. It's also the highest, coldest, greenest, and maybe the prettiest in Virginia. James Burke discovered the area in the 1740s when he followed a wounded elk there. Legend says he planted the potato peelings that provided food for the Irish surveying party that came through in 1749, who jokingly named the place "Burkes Garden." To get there, take Route 623 east and south out of Tazewell for about 15 miles.

Pocahontas Exhibition Coal Mine shows the history of the coal industry starting with the opening of the first mine in the area. Jordan Nelson discovered the coal in the early 1850s, and this area became the first and most extensively mined section of the county. This mine has been closed since 1955 (after being worked since 1883), and the town's population has dwindled to about one-third of its prime size. Clarence Ayers, a miner for twenty-seven years, stands at the gate ready to take your admission ($1.50 per adult) and talk with you before you drive your car through (it's that wide) or, better yet, walk through the 750-foot tunnel. You might want to take a sweater or jacket with you, even if it's warm outside.

The mine is open from May 1 through October 31. Take Route 102 west out of Bluefield (named for a type of chicory that has a dark blue flower and the bluegrass native to the county) and stay straight (figuratively speaking) on this road for about 9 miles. Although route signs and signs to the Pocahontas Mine are evident by their absence, you see other signs, such as "Welcome to West Virginia," signs for Nemours, Wolfe, Bramwell, and Abb's Valley, and a sign saying "Coal is not a four-letter word." Eventually you'll notice you're riding along the railroad tracks. That's a good sign. Just on the other side of Pocahontas (on Route 644), turn right over the bridge onto the railroad tracks, and the mine entrance will be on your left. Note that there is a bridge with an 8-foot, 9-inch clearance on Route 102 (slightly more clearance on the right side as you're going to Pocahontas), so check the height of your trailer or camper or luggage rack before you venture on this ride.

As you enter Pocahontas (named for the Indian princess because the town was the princess of the coal country), you'll see a huge cemetery on the right, which was started with the big mine disaster in 1882. In town you'll find the Frank and Peggy Rodri-guez Funeral Home, a Kozy Korner restaurant, an IGA general store (drygoods were removed because people were going 10 miles to the K-Mart in Bluefield), and Frankie's Dairy Bar. The City Hall/Opera House (built in 1895), a row of buildings with the original pressed metal facings and wrought iron and wooden benches, are today's reminders of yesterday. Kathleen Sayers is the postmaster in a building constructed in 1894 for the Radford Trust Company (first bank in the community), the post office, and the company doctor.

You return the same way you came, take the four-lane highway (Route 460) back to Interstate 77, or set off to get lost as you wish. For a good mental break from the winding roads, stop at the Virginia Welcome Station on Interstate 77 for one of the pret-tiest views ever seen from a welcome station in any state. The two stations at either end of Interstate 77 are done in a rustic style, while the others are done in a Colonial Williamsburg fashion.

Washington County

Probably the best-known historic and tourist area in Washing-ton County is Abingdon, the oldest incorporated town west of the Blue Ridge Mountains. It's also Virginia's largest burley tobacco market.

One of the better-known attractions in Abingdon is the world-famous **Barter Theatre** (open April through October), with comic and slightly serious traveling company presentations such as the marvelously funny *Greater Tuna* by Jaston Williams and Joe Sears. Bob Porterfield gathered the first production company to-gether during the Depression, when they bartered their presenta-tions with area residents for food and services. The seats installed in the 1950s, taken from the closed Empire Theatre on Broadway, served well but have been replaced with "new" seats from the closed Jefferson Theatre in Falls Church. Rex Partington is now the head of the theatre. The Barter Theatre is at 127 West Main Street; (703) 628-3991.

The Historic District of Abingdon is about twenty square blocks of restored 100- and 200-year-old homes and buildings, each with its own story. A self-guided–tour pamphlet is available from the

Chamber of Commerce. As examples, on East Main Stre
runs through the district, is the Tavern, a nicely restorec
rant said to be the oldest building in Abingdon (1779); th
House Craft Shop; the Abingdon General Store and Gallery, witn
crafts, gourmet goods, and a bakery; the Christmas Shoppe, with
ornate ornaments from around the world; and Loafer's Glory, a
wonderful antique store. Off the end of Valley Street is the William King Arts Center, with a gallery and eight studios of artists
and crafters. Pick up the pamphlet at the Washington County
Chamber of Commerce, 179 East Main Street, or call (703) 628–
8141.

Speaking of the Cave House, manager William Gable tells us
that this is the gathering point for 150 crafters from within 50
miles of town. Their quilts, pottery, gourmet food, sculpture, fine
art, glass, clothing, and other items are available here, in this
nineteenth-century Victorian house (279 East Main Street, (703)
628–7721). The house is open Monday through Saturday from
10:00 A.M. to 5:00 P.M. and Sunday from 1:00 P.M. to 5:00 P.M. In
January and February, the Cave House is open only on Thursday,
Friday, and Saturday.

The towns of Abingdon and nearby Damascus have *unofficially*
opened a 3.75-mile hiking and biking trail known as the **Virginia
Creeper Trail.** The 34 miles of VCT runs along an old railroad
bed from Abingdon to the North Carolina state line. This portion
of the trail begins near the corner of Green Springs Road and A
Street and continues to the Watauga Road, State Route 677.
There is an abundance of beautiful scenery, passing through
farmland, a small mountain range, and over creeks and gullies.
Thanks to the assistance of the Jacobs Creek Job Corps and the
Seabees, there are four trestle bridges, which have been floored
for pedestrian use and are provided with handrails. Motorized
vehicles, firearms, and alcoholic beverages are not permitted. The
trail passes through private property, and you are asked to remain on the trail itself and not trespass on the private property.
For additional information contact the Mount Rogers National
Recreation Area, Route 1, Box 303, Marion 24354 (703–783–
5196) or Al Bradley, Town Manager's Office, P.O. Box 789,
Abingdon 24210.

Glade Spring is the home of **Country Gourmet** restaurant,
well known locally for its mix of Mexican, early southern, southwest Virginia cuisine and "other" menu offerings. Jeff and Jo No-

lan welcome you to this 1836 historic restaurant. Your table may be an original treadle sewing machine, and you'll sit in handmade oak chairs. Around you are paintings by local artists, old prints and antiques. Highly recommended are the smoked trout (local from White's Mill) if it's available, the very nice wine list, and of course the atmosphere.

Country Gourmet is off Interstate 81 at exit 11 between Abingdon and Marion. Call (703) 429-2171.

South of town, off Route 11, is the **Tri-State Livestock Market,** the largest cattle auction house in the region. As many as 3,000 head of cattle can go through the pens during a single auction session. Spectators sit in seats from an old theatre, with room for about 200, plus standees, and watch as the cattle are brought in, weighed, and sold. Many of them will become the hamburgers you'll eat next week or month or year. The market is noisy, it can be hot in the summer, it's smelly and filled with flies, but it's exciting.

Lloyd N. Blair has been in the business for sixty years, and his son Frank is now manager. Ronald Wheatley of Nickolsville and Dan Williams from Boone, North Carolina, are the auctioneers. Lloyd Blair started Dan "as a boy" about eleven years ago, and in 1982 he won the title of World Champion Auctioneer.

They have cattle auctions every Friday morning at 9:00, except during the last two weeks of December. During the fall there are three sessions a week, with special sales on Monday at 7:30 P.M. The auctions are open to the public at no admission charge. Write P.O. Box 558, Abingdon 24210 or call (703) 628-5111.

About 5 miles north of Abingdon (turn off Main Street to Tanner, turn right on Valley Street, then left on White's Mill Road) is **White's Mill,** one of several historic mills still operating in the state. This four-story, fully waterpower-driven gristmill dates back to 1790. Guy Miller, a third-generation family member from the area, runs the mill from 9:00 A.M. to 6:00 P.M. every day, but perhaps not that many hours on Sunday. Of course, if you've never seen a water mill operate, he'll start it up for you.

You can buy fresh cornmeal here, as at most of the other mills throughout the state. Inside you'll find structural touches such as a crossbeam 30 inches high cut from one tree where you can hardly see the hewn marks. Miller will show you the non-facing side so you can see the difference between being able to see the hewn marks and not being able to. Then he'll show you the 40-

foot single-piece beam and the wooden pegs keeping the place together.

Outside the mill, there are about 100,000 nice-sized rainbow trout in an assortment of ponds that Miller nurtures so you can go out there and fish. There's a charge. This is not sport fishing, as no throwbacks are allowed, but two neighborhood cats look very well fed, and we've been told trout is a good part of their diet.

Bristol is the "twin cities" whose State Street is the dividing line between Tennessee and Virginia. A great deal of commerce and industry is located here, such as the Dixie Coca-Cola bottling plant, the Electrolux vacuum cleaner plant, and several others. Some of the plants will let you tour their operation, but you should check ahead of time.

Kern's Bakery, on the north side of Bristol at 2951 Lee Highway, offers tours through its plant, which produces bread, hot dog buns, and hamburger rolls. You get to see, up close, with all the noise, heat, and delicious smells, the dough being mixed, dumped, poked, showered, baked, cooled, and inserted into plastic bags. Tours are available weekdays except Tuesday from 8:00 A.M. to 5:00 P.M. They'd appreciate a phone call about a week in advance for large groups; small groups should call ahead but may just drop in for the tour, which will take about 30 minutes. Call (703) 669-2167.

The famed "Bristol—A Good Place to Live" sign with arrows pointing to the Virginia and Tennessee sides of State Street is right outside the Trainstation.

The Trainstation Marketplace is downtown at State and Washington streets, just east of the railroad tracks on the Virginia side.

Wise County

Coal mining is a major industry in this southwest corner (in Lee, Scott, and Wise counties), with some fourteen million tons of coal mined by about 4,500 miners in 300 different mines.

In Wise, even at night, you can see a huge and amazing coal transloader at the Westmoreland Coal Company Bullitt Mine Complex from Highway 23 and Route 68, in Appalachia. The transloader processes four to five million tons of coal per year.

The **Coal Museum** on Shawnee Avenue in Big Stone Gap is

owned by Westmoreland Coal Company and operated by Big Stone Gap Department of Parks and Recreation. The museum exhibits artifacts, painstakingly assembled from private homes and public buildings, that illustrate the coal-mining heritage of the area and coal mining's profound effect on the local lifestyle. It's open year-round on Wednesday, Thursday, Friday, and Saturday from 10:00 A.M. to 5:00 P.M., on Sunday from 1:00 P.M. to 4:00 P.M., and by appointment. Call (703) 523–4950.

For the longest continuing outdoor drama, see *The Trail of the Lonesome Pine* in Big Stone Gap, telling the story of the romance of a mountain girl during the development of the coal industry. It is adapted from a book by John Fox, Jr., and it has been presented every year since 1963. Performances are given on Thursday, Friday, and Saturday in July and August at 8:30 P.M. Call (703) 523–2060.

June Tolliver was the heroine in Fox's book, and her home is open from about Easter or some time in May through the week before Christmas for tours. Fantastic local craft offerings from the gift shop, again open only until the last week before Christmas, are a must. The **June Tolliver House** is on Highway 23.

Next door to the June Tolliver House is the Duff Academy, the one-room schoolhouse whose original school bell they ring during performances of *Lonesome Pine*. Check with Donna Bunch, the director of the Tourist and Information Center for the Gap Corporation. Her offices have been in the Duff Academy during nice weather, but she has operated out of her home during the winter because the Academy is not heated. The center is located in the "101 Interstate Railroad Car" located at the entrance of the Country Boy Motel on routes 58 and 23 in Big Stone Gap. Call (703) 523–2060.

For authentic Fox family furnishings, visit the John Fox, Jr., Museum in Big Stone Gap. The house was opened in 1970, and tours are given in the afternoon in June, July, and August by appointment. Closed Monday. Dinner for groups up to forty people is available by prearrangement. Call (703) 523–2747.

The **Southwest Virginia Museum** is in a four-story mansion bequeathed in 1946 by Congressman C. Bascom Slemp. Opened in 1947, it strives to preserve a picture of the lifestyle of the early southwest Virginia pioneers. It is open March through December: seven days a week from Memorial Day through Labor Day and closed Monday from March through Memorial Day and Labor

Day through December. The museum is located at the corner of West First Street and Wood Avenue (Route 58), just off U.S. Route 23 in Big Stone Gap. Call (703) 523–1322 for more details.

The area may look familiar for those of you who've seen the movie *Coal Miner's Daughter.* Some filming was done here.

Wythe County

The sign over the drugstore down by the train tracks in **Rural Retreat** boasts that this town was the home of pharmacist Dr. Charles T. Pepper, developer in the mid-1860s of the formula for the popular soft drink that now bears his name. Dr. Pepper was raised in nearby Christiansburg, started his medical career in Bristol, and then moved to Rural Retreat. The story goes that his daughter fell in love with his soda jerk (which did not please the good doctor). He sent her off to school and fired the soda jerk, who moved to Waco, Texas, where he again worked as a soda jerk and started making the soda mixture originally developed by Dr. Pepper. The soda became very popular with area residents, and the rest is history.

Back in town, you may want to read all about Virginia's history and the development of the area, so stop by Robert and Caroline Wing's **Blue Ridge Books,** 148 W. Main Street in Wytheville (the first syllable is pronounced "with") for a nice selection of local books. The Wings acquired the book store in April 1988. She is a retired public librarian from Wythe County. She says she just loves the shop and the different people she meets. Call (703) 228-8303.

The Wytheville State Fish Hatchery, near Fort Chiswell, grows trout for us to catch and eat in other parts of the state. Threatened with closure by the Reagan administration, the state took it over in 1984.

This hatchery (or any of several other hatcheries in the state) can boggle an angler's mind. You start this tour by viewing five aquariums. You'd expect to see tanks with fish in them, except these tanks house trout, not tropical fish. Then you move inside the hatchery building, which contains incubation equipment for the four and one-half million trout eggs laid each fall. Next to the incubators are twenty 30-foot concrete tanks, which hold the thousands of little fish (about 1 to 2 inches), all huddled together.

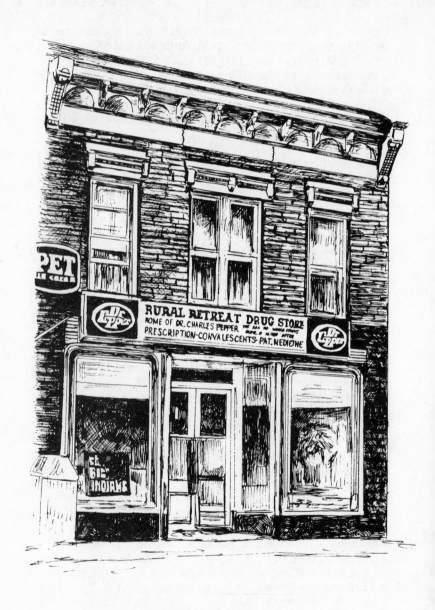

Rural Retreat Drug Store

Outside are the raceways, and each of these 100-foot-long, 8-foot-wide troughs can hold 8,000 nine-inch trout. Most of the fish are sent off to stock streams and lakes, but many are kept as breeders. These are kept up to four years, and they are huge. For a nickel you can buy trout food and watch them flock to you. (Where are they when you have a trout line in hand?) After age four, when they're about 6 pounds, they're taken to streams and rivers throughout the northeast to grow to 10 to 12 pounds for that "trophy"-size catch.

The Hatchery is 12 miles from Wytheville. Take exit 25 off Interstate 81, go south on Route 52 for 1 mile, then left on Route 629 for about 2 miles, and it will be on your left.

Colonel John Chiswell discovered lead and zinc deposits in this area about 1757 while he was hiding from the Cherokees. From those deposits, shot was made for firearms for frontiersmen and settlers at the **shot tower.** This is one of only three such towers in the United States. Thomas Jackson built the tower around 1807. The walls are $2^{1}/_{2}$ feet thick, with a 20-foot square base. Inside the tower, you'll see how lead was dropped from the pouring kettle sieve at the top of the 70-foot tower to a kettle of cold water 75 feet below ground. The 145-foot fall and cold water dunking formed the shot into hardened round balls.

The shot tower is open daily from 10:00 A.M. to 6:00 P.M. Memorial Day through Labor Day and weekends in April, May, September, and October. Admission to the tower is 75 cents for adults and 50 cents for children. It's a climb. Off Interstate 77 at the Poplar Camp exit, go $1^{1}/_{2}$ miles west on Route 52 to the park entrance. Call (804) 674–5492 for the schedule.

Off the Beaten Path in Shenandoah Virginia

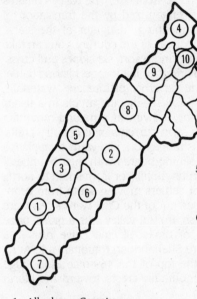

1. Alleghany County
   Humpback Covered Bridge
   Gathright Dam and Lake
   Moomaw
2. Augusta County
   Museum of American
   Frontier Culture
   Belle Grae Bed and
   Breakfast and Bistro
   Wright's Dairy Rite
   Statler Brothers Complex
   Natural Chimneys
   Candy Shop
3. Bath County
   Garth Newel
   The Homestead
   Falling Springs
4. Frederick County
   Clearbrook Woolen Shop
   Wayside Inn
   Manuel's and Wife

5. Highland County
   Little Highland Maple
   Museum
   Campbell House
6. Roanoke County
   Virginia Museum of
   Transportation
   Hotel Roanoke
   Shogun restaurant
   Mary Bladon House
7. Rockbridge County
   Virginia Horse Center
   James River and Kanawha
   Canal
   Lime Kiln Arts Theater at
   the Kiln
   Goshen Pass
   Fassifern Bed and
   Breakfast
8. Rockingham County
   Daniel Harrison House
9. Shenandoah County
   Shenandoah Valley Music
   Festival
   Tuttle & Spice General
   Store Museum
   Strasburg
   Bob and Peg's Vintage
   Village
   Meems Bottom Bridge
10. Warren County
    Apple House

Shenandoah Virginia

The Shenandoah Valley stretches from the northwestern corner of the state down 200 miles to Roanoke. The valley conjures all sorts of romantic pictures, epitomized by the translation of *Shenandoah,* an Indian word meaning "daughter of the stars." Here, in one of the most scenic areas of the country, you can take your pick of covered bridges, a grand resort, ski slopes and cross-country skiing, the brilliant colorings of fall foliage, historic battlefields, deep natural limestone caverns, picturesque waterfalls, hiking through inviting natural forests, dipping a pole in a fishin' hole, exploring rustic log cabins, a swim in a natural mountain lake, whitewater rafting along swift currents, and country crafts. The Shenandoah Valley's crops range from vineyards to apples to maple syrup and fill many groaning boards with their bounties.

The valley, where the river runs "uphill," or from south to north, was the main thoroughfare for settlers moving south from Pennsylvania. More than seventy percent of the Civil War battles were fought in Virginia, and this lush, fruitful valley was a grand prize that changed hands dozens of times. Skyline Drive runs 105 miles through the 194,000-acre Shenandoah National Park. At its southern end it meets with the top of the 469-mile Blue Ridge Parkway as it winds along mountain crests toward the North Carolina border.

The valley is a monument to history and beauty. But it is also new and modern and exciting. The new multi-million–dollar Virginia Horse Center is destined to be a major part of our country's horse culture. And the new $170 million Adolph Coors Company plant sits near the South Fork of the Shenandoah River. After some contentious beginnings, Coors seems to have become a good neighbor. In addition to becoming Rockingham County's biggest taxpayer, Coors has made a significant community contribution. They have pledged $150,000 to Rockingham Memorial Hospital's new cancer center, employed 305 local people, and organized an employee group for local volunteer work. Their recurring public relations theme is "Getting Together With Virginia," and it appears that most people approve of its desire to be a good citizen.

At the southern terminus is Roanoke, the cultural center of the valley with its outstanding art, science, history, and transportation museums.

Alleghany County

The **Humpback Covered Bridge,** a graceful, arched span erected in 1835 just west of Covington, is said to be the only bridge of this type in the country and perhaps in the world, although apparently three of them were originally built within a mile of each other. It received its name because of a rise of 8 feet from the ends to the center. It has no center support. Reportedly, Thomas Kincaid, an eighteen-year-old, using an ax as his principal tool, cut the hand-hewn timbers and made the locust pins that join the timbers. No nails were used. The structure was part of the James River/Kanawha Turnpike, apparently saved from destruction by an unwritten agreement between the Confederate and Union soldiers during the Civil War.

The 100-foot, single-span walled structure over Dunlop Creek carried traffic for nearly 100 years before being abandoned in 1929 and for nearly a quarter of a century stood a derelict near its then modern successor. Since 1954 it has been maintained as a part of a five-acre highway wayside 3 miles west of Covington on Highway 60. At the wayside are several picnic tables, barbecue grills, and two portable toilets, and you can wade through the creek for a better, or at least a different, view of the bridge. Several Civil War cannon balls have been found in the creek and along its banks, as both Union and Confederate troops moved across the bridge with cannons. Graffiti artists have used the walls and roof of the bridge as their canvas, but none of the words seem too objectionable, mostly love notes from the young at heart and the young at mind.

Unlike most other covered bridges in the state, which take a detailed map to find, this one is easy to locate: there are signs off Interstate 64 at exit 3, Callaghan Interchange, directing you to the Humpback. You can also get there by traveling west out of Covington for about 3 miles.

Thomas M. Gathright, Sr., a landowner, farmer, and avid sportsman, and Benjamin C. Moomaw, Jr., executive director of the Covington-Alleghany County Chamber of Commerce, championed the cause for the construction of a water control project on the Jackson River to protect Covington and other downriver communities from flooding. In their honor are **Gathright Dam** and **Lake Moomaw.** The 12-mile-long lake, with its 43.5 miles of shoreline, was created by a dam that is 1,310 feet long and rises 257 feet above the Jackson River bed. Wanda Warlitner says the

Humpback Covered Bridge

dam's appearance is misleading, particularly if you've seen any of the monumental projects such as Hoover Dam. It's a clay and rock structure, and you can drive over it, and it just looks like another piece of shoreline. It's set amid this gorgeous country-side, and during the thirty to forty-five minutes it takes to get there you feel like you're driving to the top of the world. Many people, says Wanda, ask, "Where's the dam?" It isn't until you go into the visitors center and see the display and then go outside to the overlook that you realize the water at the dam is 150 feet deep (the lake has an average depth of 80 feet).

The visitors center is open 8:30 A.M. to 4:00 P.M. and has some interesting information. Wanda and Bill Whit (Bill's the dam oper-ator, with the project since it was started in 1967) will answer your questions. Except one: Wanda says she doesn't know why the water is green; although lots of people ask, no one seems to have an answer. The room downstairs is used periodically for classes and lectures, and they're hoping it will hold displays and be used more frequently in the future.

Camping in the Gathright Dam and Lake Moomaw area is available in several U.S. Forest Service camping areas on a first-come, first-served basis for $5 a night (Golden Eagle is half price). Obviously, there are some peak times when the whoosh of a dog's wagging tail couldn't squeeze into the campgrounds, partic-ularly during fall foliage. However, Wanda says the Morris Hill camping area, with its fifty-five campsites and dumpsite, potable water, and restroom buildings, about a forty-five-minute drive from recreational facilities at Lake Moomaw, doesn't always fill up when the leaves are changing.

For additional information, write to the James River Ranger District, 313 South Monroe Ave., Covington 24426, or call (703) 962-2214. The dam and lake are about 10 miles north of Coving-ton. Take Route 220 to Route 687, to Route 641, to Route 666, which will bring you to the facilities. One of the alternative routes to or from Gathright Dam and Lake Moomaw is via Route 605. This is a rough gravel and dirt road (one of the major understate-ments of the decade, if not the century). It's not recommended for towed or recreational vehicles.

Augusta County

The newest museum in the Staunton (pronounced *Stanton*)· area is the **Museum of American Frontier Culture,** the only one of its kind in the world. The concept was proposed in 1975, and it called for a major international center of significant educational, cultural, and economic impact. Assistance and support was received from many historical and cultural organizations and groups on a local and international level.

The museum was charged with collecting, accurately reconstructing, and demonstrating four working nineteenth-century farmsteads. Two of them were brought to the site from European nations the pioneers had left behind them, Northern Ireland and Germany, and the English farm was reconstructed (it couldn't be removed because of English preservation law). It is said that although the countless stones that made up the Irish farmhouse were numbered in place, somehow they multiplied like so many wire hangers, and quite a few were left over after it was reassembled here in the States.

The fourth farmstead was donated by Phyllis Riddlebarger of Botetourt County, Virginia, reflecting the melding of European influences. Her late husband's grandparents bought the farm in 1884. You can see the adaptations in the German V-notched log barn construction, and the A-frame roofed smokehouse has English derivations. The center will also amass and preserve archival and genealogical collections and artifacts. Historical research, academic outreach, intern programs, and the preparation of appropriate materials and publications will play a vital role in the museum programs.

The American and Irish farmsteads are the only ones completed so far, with the English estate due for completion in early 1991 and the German farm in 1990. A visitor center will also be added.

The museum is located at the junction of Interstates 64 and 81; admission is $4 for adults and $2 for children. When it opened in September 1988, the visiting hours were daily from 9:00 A.M. to 5:00 P.M. For further information write the museum at P.O. Box 810, Staunton 24401 or call (703) 332–7850.

On display in the Staunton firehouse on Augusta Street is Jumbo, a fire engine acquired in 1911 and lovingly restored by Billy Thompson's White Post Restorations (see Clarke County). Stop by during the day and the fire fighters on duty will show you into the room, or if you come at night you can look through the windows. Souvenir tumblers ($7) are available, and because they still owe a considerable portion of the $143,000 it cost to restore the fire truck, they'll accept donations. Call (703) 886–0803 for further details.

Staunton has a different festival every month, so there's almost always something happening in this very vibrant town. Check with the Staunton-Augusta County Chamber of Commerce, 30 North New Street, Staunton 24401 or call (703) 886–2351 for detailed tourism information.

Ken Hicks (with his dog, Bellboy) and Michael Organ run the **Belle Grae Bed and Breakfast and Bistro** at 515 West Frederick Street, a restored 1870 house (some chandeliers and other pieces are original). Mike is the innkeeper and delights in telling the history of the home, named for the two mountains, Betsy Belle and Mary Grae, visible from the front door. Mike says a happy resident ghost, perhaps former owner Mrs. Bagby, lives somewhere between the second and third floors, but generally only visits during large festive events and entertainments.

Ken runs the food side of the business, providing for large dinner parties and receptions with such house favorites as baked yellowtail with red pepper sauce, charbroiled scallops, a lot of pork, chocolate peanut butter pie (not generally served in the summertime) or buttermilk pie (similar to chess pie), creole soup (in Ken's family for generations and they don't give out the recipe, but he uses a beef fat base with tomatoes, green peas, and celery but no seafood) that he will serve as a soup or as a sauce over prime rib, and cheese grits. Dinners are served Tuesday through Saturday, with brunch on Sunday. Reservations are essential. Where the Belle Grae is of Federalist style covered by a 1918 revision to Italianate, the bistro is art deco. Call (703) 886–5151 for reservations.

The **Virginia Made Store,** owned by Terry and Ginger LeMasurier, features a wide collection of Virginia products including Pruden's hams ($2.25 a pound), Pruden's bacon, wines, crafts, colonial gifts and accessories and souvenirs. They do a particularly good Christmas craft business. Many of the crafts appear more modern than traditional, but there is a variety of things such as cornhusk dolls, cornhusk flowers, grapevine and pinecone wreaths and cotton rugs, the best-selling item in the shop. Everything promotes Virginia, and almost everything is made in Virginia except some souvenirs made elsewhere in the United States (they couldn't find Virginia manufacturers for some of these items). Nothing is foreign-made. About half of the artists are from the Staunton area. This shop has been open since early 1984, and Terry is hoping to open another one in the old Market Place in Roanoke. Write for a catalog at Route 4, Box 90-1, Staunton, 24401, or call (703) 886-7180. To get to the shop, take Route 250 east of Staunton at Interstate 81.

Wright's Dairy Rite (703-886-0435) at 346 Greenville Avenue (Route 11) may be the last (or one of the last) curb-service hamburger joints, where you order from the speaker on your "Servusfone" at your parking place. F. A. Wright started it in 1952 and insisted that only the highest quality and freshest ingredients be used in his kitchen. Mr. Wright created a tradition in Staunton that has existed for over thirty years. To this day Wright's is still family-owned (Mr. and Mrs. Cash own it now). Reportedly this is where the Statler Brothers used to hang out and perhaps where they started composing one or more of their songs. On the menu is the Superburger, two patties of pure ground beef, tangy melted cheese, shredded lettuce and their own special sauce all on a specially baked three-decker bun for $1.40. The milkshakes (chocolate, vanilla, strawberry, cherry, pineapple, banana, butterscotch, raspberry) are $.90 and the malted milkshake is $1.

You can visit the **Statler Brothers Complex** (703-885-7297), housed in the restored Beverley Manor grade school, to see memorabilia and look through the gift shop. It's open Monday through Friday, 10:30 A.M. to 3:30 P.M., with a free guided tour at 2:00 P.M. Large groups should call ahead for tour arrangements. It's located on Thornrose Avenue near Gypsy Hill Park.

The **Natural Chimneys** regional park area in Mt. Solon is the home of some towering limestone structures—impressive scenery indeed. Two annual jousting tournaments have been taking place here for about 165 years. The jousting started in 1821 with two men deciding who should have a damsel for his wife. You can view the drama of medieval competition during the Hall of Fame Joust on the third weekend of June. The August weekend features local crafters as well as the tournaments, and it draws a larger crowd. A few thousand people turn out for the one-day events, a combination of horsemanship, balance, and marksmanship. Some jousters use lances a hundred years old.

Tour the Jousting Hall of Fame, which features the history of the sport at Natural Chimneys and about fifty of the best and most important men and women in the sport. Trophies, brass plates with the names of champions engraved upon them, and testimony to the jousters' accomplishments fill the displays. To qualify, a member must have a minimum of twenty years of involvement in jousting, have promoted jousting on a national level, made special contributions, and won titles. Talk with Park Manager Carl Vance or Park Ranger Rob Houle. Camping, 120 sites with water and electricity, is available for $12 a night, which includes your admission into the Chimneys area.

Normally, admission to the Chimneys is $3 per car, but for the jousting days it's $2 for adults and $1 for children. You can't see the chimneys from the jousting grounds, but they're only 100 yards away. Natural Chimneys is just north of Mt. Solon on Route 721. Call (703) 350–2510 for details.

Jason and Patricia Weaver opened the **Candy Shop** a few years ago in the old schoolhouse, selling gifts and Hershey products made at the Stuarts Draft Hershey factory. They became so successful that they constructed their own building, a country cottage affair, a few blocks down the road. Now they sell quilts, local handmade furniture, punched tin, all 57 varieties made by Heinz, and San Giorgio (Hershey products). They have a custom quilt operation, so you can order your pattern and color and material, and one of eight Mennonite women including Pat (from Indiana, Ohio, Pennsylvania, and Virginia) will create your quilt. The pieces are machine stitched as much as possible, but all quilting is done by hand. A king-size quilt costs about $425, with most quilts running about $350 to $500. Another Amish lady, says Pat, has two looms and makes rugs and placemats. The award-winning 1584 piece-stuffed square quilt mentioned in previous editions of *Viginia: Off the Beaten Path* is still on display in the loft, and other distinguished quilts are on display on a rotation basis. The Candy Shop is at 10 Highland Drive and is open Monday through Saturday from 10:00 A.M. to 5:00 P.M. Go through the traffic light at Route 608, and it is a little farther on your left. The phone number is (703) 337–1438.

Not too far away is Kinsinger's Bakery, "where everything is made from scratch". Cakes, cookies, salads, jams, breads, rolls, cinnamon rolls, and pies are available hot out of the oven. The aromas alone could draw you from miles away. Kinsinger's Kountry Kitchen is on Route 651 off of Route 608. It's open Thursday, Friday, and Saturday from 9:00 A.M. to 5:00 P.M. but closed January and February. (703) 337–2668.

Half a mile away (one mile north of Stuarts Draft's only traffic light on Route 608 is The Cheese Shop, offering twenty-five varieties of cheese, free samples, dried fruits, nuts, natural snacks and bulk foods, real butter, Lebanon bologna, and no-sugar apple butter. The Cheese Shop is open from 9:00 A.M. to 5:30 P.M. (Saturdays 9:00 A.M. to 5:00 P.M.) and closed Wednesday and Sunday. The phone number is (703) 337-4224.

All three of these shops are owned by Mennonite families.

Bath County

The people of Bath County boast that there are no traffic lights in the county, no billboards (there are advertising signs on the roads, but no "billboards"), and because the weather is cool enough, there are no mosquitoes. We must admit that in our travels through this area we have never met a mosquito in Bath County. What Bath has to offer is lots of pretty scenery, some of the oldest rock formations known to geology, and a few pleasant ways to spend some time.

Warm Springs is the county seat and home to the Bath County Historical Museum (created in 1969 and open weekdays from June through October) and the courthouse with its monument to the Confederate soldier. The Chamber of Commerce and the school board share facilities in an old schoolhouse.

Arlene and Luca Di Cecco, violinist and cellist, respectively, operate **Garth Newel** (Welsh for "new home"), Virginia's only center for studying and performing chamber music. She is from South Africa and was educated in London. He is from Connecticut; they met in Rome when he was there as a Fulbright Scholar. Between Warm Springs and Hot Springs, on 114 acres, with the Allegheny Mountains as a background, you can hear concerts featuring string quartets or a piano trio or sometimes as many as an octet, with Paul Nitsch as pianist and harpsichordist in residence. They are performed every Sunday at 3:00 P.M. and almost every Saturday evening at 5:00 P.M. from July 4 through Labor Day. Lighter compositions are performed at the Fourth of July and Labor Day events. In the summer, the performances are held on the stage of Herter Hall. Students sometimes participate in these programs and can also be heard throughout the area at other events in local churches. In the winter, the venue moves to the manor house living room, and guests enjoy gourmet meals, country lodging, and fireside concerts. Several spring and fall holiday music weekends are scheduled, and guests can stay for the entire weekend or find lodging elsewhere in the vicinity. Weekend visits are about $70 or $80 per person per night including dinner and concert, with accommodations for about twenty people. Concerts only are about $40. Reservations are sometimes made a year in advance, particularly for Thanksgiving weekend, but definitely should be made at least two months ahead of time (703–839–5018). Garth Newel is a nonprofit operation and is sponsored by contributions, donations, and matching grants from arts organizations.

Daughter Mila Di Cecco operates the Squire's Table restaurant on Route 220, just 8 miles south of Hot Springs, which features continental food described as imaginative, traditional cuisine with fresh ingredients featuring a strong Italian influence. It is set in an old log cabin with a stone fireplace and old plates. The Squire's Table is open for dinner from Wednesday through Sunday and lunch on weekends during the summer.

West of Warm Springs and west of West Warm Springs on Route 687, 1 mile down the road, is **Bacova** (*BA*th *CO*unty *Vir*gini*A*), a town with a tale. (On the way you'll pass Webb's General Store, an emporium founded in 1905 where the motto's been "if we haven't got it you don't need it.") Originally a company town where Tidewater Oil Company oil barrel parts were made, Bacova and its forty-two cottages were purchased in 1957 by Malcolm Hirsh (whose father reportedly wrote the Boola Boola song for Yale) for the huge sum of $125,000. He painted the 1920–1922 cottages pretty pastels and, with the assistance of Grace Boulton Gilmore of New Bern, North Carolina, started a new cottage industry in the abandoned warehouse. She had been working with resins and fiberglass, after hand painting ties and bathrobes for some of the better stores across the country. The Bacova Guild, started in 1965, now has a line of fifty different items, including the popular cardinal-adorned mailboxes, thermometers, trash cans, kindling cans, and other home accessories.

Hirsh has since sold the operation to former tennis pros Pat Haynes and Ben Johns, but this quaint town of cottages, one church, and a "factory" is a delightful sight to behold. Wind chimes hanging from cottage porches sound their song on a cool fall afternoon. Neighbors join each other in rocking chairs or on porch swings before the supper activities start. Children play in the crotch of an old fruit tree. No wonder Bath County doesn't feel the need for lots of organized recreational activities.

Bacova Guild Showroom is an outlet store that can really save you some money on Bacova products. Located in the old Watson Building in Hot Springs, the showroom also carries a line of golfing things, and other crafts. Additionally, you can now find Bacova Guild items in your L. L. Bean catalogue, K-Mart, and Hechingers (of course, the chain store product is mass-produced and made of galvanized steel, not fiberglass). It has grown so much it is listed as 374th on *Inc.* magazine's list of 500 fastest-growing private companies nationwide.

Bath County may be best known for **The Homestead** at Hot Springs, one of those venerable resorts dating back for what seems forever. It's set on some 15,000 acres, offers three golf courses (one designed by Robert Trent Jones), numerous tennis courts, warm baths, swimming pools, bowling, skiing, ice skating, horseback riding, carriages, stream fishing, children's activities, and countless other amenities. Five men wait on you at your dinner table, your bed is turned down at night (discreetly, while you're at dinner), and chocolates await your retiring. The stars shine most brightly on the kitchen and its chef and pastry chef, for no matter what you order, it's done to perfection. Playing golf in this area can be devastating to your ego. The courses are tough, but some say it's the magnificent view that's so distracting to your concentration. The combination tends to add a few strokes to your average score.

Although not inexpensive (no one would expect it to be), you can sometimes book into packages, such as golfing, wine tasting, tennis, or skiing, which will reduce the overall price. You can stay at the nearby Cascades, which is owned by the Homestead, for a little less and pay a nominal premium to dine at the Homestead or use some of its facilities. As can be expected, fall foliage is a busy time, and you could have trouble getting a shadow in this place without prior reservations. Occupancy is lighter in July and August. Call (703) 839–5500.

A little farther south on Route 220 is **Falling Springs,** a leaping cascade of about 200 feet noted by Thomas Jefferson in his book *Notes on Virginia,* written in 1781. A sign cautions you that Route 220 is heavily traveled and that you should be careful as you walk from the nearby parking area to the falls. Be careful.

The Homestead

Take your camera and maybe look for some afternoon sun or early morning mist. It's beautiful.

North of the scenic byway known as Route 39, the Virginia Power Company's **Bath County Pumped Storage Project** sits like a new world out of a science fiction film. On one side of the mountain it backs up the Big Back Creek, and on the other side it dams up Little Back Creek. One lake is higher in elevation than the other. Water is released from the upper storage area through pipes that are 1000 feet long and 28$^1/_2$ feet in diameter, and on through the turbines to generate electricity. At night, or when there's less demand on electricity, the turbines are reversed and the water is pumped from the bottom reservoir to the top. Thus, the only water loss is due to evaporation. The Storage Project is the largest of its type in this country. Because the water levels can fluctuate up to 60 feet in a short time, there are no recreational lake activities allowed.

A recreation area is open for camping, fishing, swimming, non-power boating, picnicking, volleyball court, horseshoes, basketball, and other activities. The day use charge is $1 for parking, and the camping is $5 a night. There are no electric hookups, but there are a comfort station with hot water showers and a trailer dumping station.

A visitors center is open seven days a week from mid-March to mid-November, usually from 10:00 A.M. to 4:30 P.M., but hours tend to be later as the days are longer. Advance reservation tours are available by calling (703) 279-3289. Although the center is handicapped accessible, walkers should wear walking shoes and not high heels.

Frederick County

Clearbrook Woolen Shop, just south of the West Virginia border, is yards off Interstate 81 at exit 83. Here you'll find a marvelous collection of yard goods and sewing needs, such as wooden purse handles, Ultrasuede belts, wallpaper to coordinate with fabrics, ribbon for edgings and belt coverings, and Schnetz sewing machine needles (Schnetz manufactures the needles that other companies then put their labels on).

William H. Lawrence II bought a woolen mill in 1930, which operated until 1970. During that time the mill produced fine

woolen yard goods and thousands and thousands of army blankets for the war. Mr. Lawrence opened the shop in 1944 in an
authentic log cabin that was earlier an old tavern from 100 miles
south of Clearbrook and that he had moved for that purpose.

William H. Lawrence III now runs the operation, which brings
in fabrics from across this and several European countries. Some
of the materials come from exclusive garment houses in New
York. He and his wife travel frequently to New York and Atlanta to
secure the newest fabrics, many of which can't be found in any
other fabric store. The Lawrences say they have the largest variety of material around and perhaps more woolens than anyone
on the East Coast. Customers come from many states, and the
shop's mailing list tops 83,000. (The largest single order was
1,500 to 1,600 yards for a coordinated fall-winter wardrobe.) Frequent instructional seminars attract several hundred attendees
and have to be held at the nearby school. Clearbrook is open
Monday through Saturday from 9:00 A.M. to 5:00 P.M. Write P.O.
Box 8, Clearbrook 22624 or call (703) 662-3442.

America's oldest motor inn, Middletown's **Wayside Inn,** had
been in operation since 1797, when it was known as Wilkerson's
Tavern, and was a marvelous place to dine and stay in one of
their twenty-one rooms. The furnishings made the place an antique lover's paradise, and manager Margie Alcarese had an-
nounced plans to hire someone to date and catalog the antiques
and artifacts. Unfortunately, on October 3, 1985, part of the inn
was destroyed in an early morning blaze. Fortunately, a goodly
portion of the antiques, including a huge painting of the Battle of
Cedar Creek, was saved, and a large collection of antiques of
equal value and beauty was safely stored off the premises.

A meal in the Lord Fairfax Room or the Slave's Quarters (both
favorites), a walk through the inn with Mary Jane Adams, func-
tions manager, or an extended stay is always a pleasure. It's located at 7783 Main Street in Middletown, (703) 869-1797. To
reach the Wayside from Interstate 81, take the Middletown exit
(exit 77) and follow signs to the Wayside Inn.

On Route 11, 5¹/₃ miles north of Stephens City, is the site of
the Battle of Kernstown, the only battle in which Stonewall Jackson was defeated (8,000 Federals against Jackson's 3,500 Confed-
erates). Although there are buildings on the road front of the
property, you can see the back portions where the battle of
March 23, 1862, took place. You can pull into the parking lot of

the Apple Blossom Motor Hotel to read more about the battle. And while you're in the Apple Blossom Motor Lodge parking lot, stop in at the restaurant run by Manuel and Florine Sempeles. It's called **Manuel's and Wife,** and it's filled with antiques, such as a spinning wheel, a display of straight-edged razors, and a book of fabric samples, that look more like decorations than old things in a museum. Some new oil paintings also decorate the walls. It's very charming.

Highland County

Once you've driven through Highland County, you understand what it means to be the third least populated county east of the Mississippi. There's an estimated ratio of five or six sheep to every person living here. Monterey, the county seat, is 50 miles and four mountains away, via winding, twisting Route 250, from Staunton.

This is maple sugar country, as testified to by the **Little Highland Maple Museum** on the outskirts of Monterey. Take a clockwise trip around this open-air museum to learn the history of maple syrup and sugar making and the tools, equipment, and processes used to make them. The museum was created in 1983 by the Highland County Chamber of Commerce and is open from 9:00 A.M. to 6:00 P.M. daily. Come spring, particularly the last two weeks in March, it's time for buckwheat cakes and maple syrup, and you can find them in any restaurant in the area.

In town, stop by the **Campbell House,** a museum with antique tools, farm implements, and furniture, as well as wool tartan scarves from Scotland, blankets, hand-crafted creations, and the finest fabrics at the Highland Wools shop. The house was built in 1855 and was a Civil War hospital in 1862. Open daily 10:00 A.M. to 5:00 P.M. or by appointment; call (703) 468–2161.

Driving from Monterey toward Staunton on Highway 250, you'll pass the scene of the Battle of McDowell, where you can view Confederate breastworks (low barriers to protect gunners). A forest walk entrance leads to an area where in 1862 a military action brought Confederate troops to this mountaintop to build fortifications that would block Union advances into the Shenandoah Valley. So effective were these fortifications that it would be 1864 before Union troops would try again to enter the valley.

Over a century later, the trenches of these wartime fortifications are visible. A short ³/₁₀-mile loop trail (about a twenty-minute walk that's a little steep and rocky in places) is marked. Travel on the forest walk is one-way and is for the foot traveler only. Three exhibit points along the way tell the story of this small part of Civil War history.

Further eastward on Highway 250 in the Jennings Branch Valley, around Churchville (named because of all the churches), about 4 miles west of Staunton, is the area where John Trimble was killed in 1764 in the last Indian raid in Augusta County.

Roanoke County

Roanoke (at one time, possibly *Rawrenock* or *Roenoak,* an Indian word meaning "white shell beads" or, more literally translated, "money") is the largest Virginia city west of Richmond. A huge neon star atop Mill Mountain, reportedly the country's largest manufactured star, was erected by the Chamber of Commerce in 1949. Mill Mountain is within the city limits, and it's said to be the only mountain in Virginia, and perhaps east of Phoenix, that's located inside a city.

Start your tour at the Market Square area in the middle of downtown. Valley farmers have been bringing their fresh fruits, vegetables, and flowers to this Roanoke market for over 100 years; now the City Market Building has been opened as a market place, and the daylight hours at these facilities and the Center-in-the-Square (see below) are excitingly vibrant. One of the more celebrated activities is the mid-October Harvest Festival, which has included a scarecrow workshop led by noted "scarecrow-ologist" Mark Baron. For those who have fond memories or not-so-fond memories, and for those whose only memory of a scarecrow is from the *Wizard of Oz,* this is the place to be. It's sponsored by the Science Museum of Western Virginia (703–342–5710).

Jan Quitsau is the executive director of the Roanoke Valley Convention and Visitors Bureau, and he and his staff can provide extraordinary amounts of information for you. Write him at P.O. Box 1710, Roanoke 24008 or call (703) 342–6025.

The Virginia Museum of Transportation, the official transportation museum of Virginia, is the South's largest collection of steam locomotives, cars, boats, airplanes, and missiles. What might excite your imagination is the H-O–gauge railroad with 1,400 feet of track, 100 turnouts, and assembly yards and structures set on 1,200 square feet. It's all computer controlled. You can board a three-car passenger train on a 7½-inch–gauge track for a half-mile ride through the museum grounds. There's a gift shop on the premises with railroad memorabilia including hats, goggles, belt buckles, handkerchiefs, patches, pins, recordings, photographs, books, puzzles, train sets, whistles, mugs, decals, and postcards.

The Virginia Museum of Transportation (303 Norfolk Avenue, 703–342–5670) is open from 10:00 A.M. to 5:00 P.M. Monday through Saturday and from noon to 5:00 P.M. Sunday. Admission is $3 for ages nineteen and over, $2 for ages thirteen to eighteen, and $1.75 for ages three to twelve.

Center-in-the-Square is a combination hands-on science museum and planetarium, art museum, history museum, and theatre. All these components are housed in a 1914 warehouse, and you can see pictures of the old warehouse and the neighborhood in the historical section. Everything is wrapped around a five-story atrium, where a spiral staircase symbolizes how these organizations have come together to create a richer cultural life in western Virginia.

The **Hotel Roanoke** was built on a ten-acre knoll overlooking the city in 1882 for $45,000. It was constructed in the Tudor style with hand-rubbed English walnut, carved oak, cherry, and ash woods; gaslight chandeliers; and floors polished to shine like glass. Much of the original Honduras mahogany remains. As with many wooden structures, part of the hotel burned in 1898. It was the first hotel in Roanoke to have bathrooms with a porcelain or zinc tub, and the first sewer line in town ran from the hotel. Telephones with multiple plugs (so you could move them around the rooms) were installed in 1931. It also featured closets with lights that turned on automatically when the door was opened, electric fans, full-length mirrors, and running ice water, and in 1937 it became one of the first hotels in the world to be air-conditioned. The swimming pool was installed in 1957 and covered in 1960.

The Hotel Roanoke brochure says it has been the premier hostelry from its opening day in December 1882, and even after a short stay you'll agree. It tells of traditional charm, grand chandeliers, deep pile carpets, and plush appointments. This probably is one of the few hotel brochures that really tells the truth. Chef Michael Klein comes from the Culinary Institute of America, two years' study at Salsburg's Mozart Hotel, the incomparable Midnight Sun restaurant in Atlanta, the Hilton on the Virgin Islands, and the Hilton Melbourne in Florida. Try his Blue Ridge Salad featuring all manner of foodstuff grown in Virginia. Weekend getaways cost $200 for two people, including continental breakfast. Call the hotel at (703) 343–6992, (800) 542–5898 (in Virginia) or (800) 336–9684 (out of state).

As the cultural center of the Shenandoah Valley, it seems somehow appropriate that you can find a Japanese restaurant here. Willis Yang owns the **Shogun restaurant,** which made headlines in 1988 as the first place to serve sushi in southwest Virginia. It also made headlines because the experienced sushi chef, Sen-tien Lee, is a Taiwanese immigrant whose future here is uncertain. Yang tried to find someone local, but he says that it is "very hard to find" an American sushi chef in this area—a mild understatement.

The **Mary Bladon House** apparently is the first home to be opened as a bed and breakfast in Roanoke. It's a ten-room Victorian home, and the first two guest rooms were opened July 1985, with two more opened in October. Owner Sally D. Pfister says the home is within walking distance of the Virginia Museum of Transportation and Center-in-the-Square. It's located at 381 Washington Ave., S.W. Call (703) 344–5361.

Rockbridge County

The Lexington Visitors Bureau has opened a new and expanded Visitor Center, which, with many furnishings and finishings donated by local businesses, is located in the Centel Telephone Company building (102 East Washington Street). Tour counselors are waiting to assist you and provide brochures, directions, and a warm welcome. Sofas and chairs are available so you can sit awhile and review the material you've received. Displays and exhibits describe the area attractions, and a slide show highlights the events of the area. Another super feature is that the entire center, including restrooms, now is handicapped accessible. For further information, call (703) 463–3777.

Lexington, Virginia, may rival Lexington, Kentucky, as the new horse center of the country, with the creation of the **Virginia Horse Center,** just north of Lexington. The center holds major horse sales, 4-H horse-judging competitions, grand prix jumping, dressage exhibitions, and breed shows.

About 4 miles east of the visitors center out Route 60 east at the Ben Salem Wayside Park are remains of the 1840 **James River and Kanawha Canal.** Conceived by George Washington as part of a "Great Central American Waterway from the Rockies to the Atlantic Ocean," this was the earliest canal system in the western hemisphere. When the canal was complete in 1854, ships could navigate from the harbors of the Atlantic coast via river to Buchanan, a distance of 197½ miles. The wayside is a delightful place for a picnic or a quiet afternoon watching the waters frolic over the river rocks.

Battery Creek Lock in Lexington is on the James River at Big Island, where the Blue Ridge Parkway passes over the river. Restored and maintained by the National Park Service, the site is complete with a visitors center housing exhibits portraying life on the canals in the mid-nineteenth century.

Lime Kiln Arts Theater at the Kiln is Lexington's newest outdoor theater. During the summer, this professional theater brings Shakespeare, *Stonewall Country* (an original musical drama based on the life of Stonewall Jackson, by Virginians) and concerts.

Where master stonemasons once plied their trade and kilns burned red-hot with the making of lime, where stars stud the skies as well as the stage, and where you can come dressed casually and comfortably (sweaters might be necessary for the cool evenings) is where you'll find these performances. Picnicking is welcome and you can either pack your own or call (703) 463-3074 to have one of the restaurants in town pack it for you. Tickets range from $8 to $10 for plays, with Tuesday nights half price. Concert tickets range from $3 to $12. (Senior citizens and children under twelve receive a $2 discount, except on Tuesdays.) Donations are accepted by this nonprofit organization, and the facilities are handicapped accessible. Take Highway 60 west out of Lexington, turn left at Route 555 to Theater at Lime Kiln. Their address is P.O. Box 663, Lexington 24450, and their phone number is (703) 463-7088.

One of Virginia's scenic byways, or roads that offer important scenic values, is Route 39 northwest of Lexington, off of Interstates 81 and 64. It's the road through **Goshen Pass,** 3 miles with jagged cliffs towering a thousand feet on either side, necklaced by dogwood, ferns and mosses, hemlock, laurel, maples, mountain ash, pines, and rhododendron. A scenic overlook (built during the repairs from the flood of November 1985) has plenty of parking places, and a picnic area is just yards away. The road passes former health spas and the Rockbridge Baths Post Office, where Lucille Reed has been the postmaster for some thirty years, and continues into the high Alleghenies of Bath County, to the Pumped Storage Project and the West Virginia border, a total of about 50 miles from Lexington.

Those who have been this way will pooh-pooh the pass as "ruined" since the November floods, but don't worry. Surely, these rocks and trees have been moved and nudged before, and those from generations ago might have a different view of today's pass.

At the entrance to Route 39, is the **Fassifern Bed and Breakfast,** as good a starting point as you could wish for for your trip through the pass. Pat and Jim Tichenor have restored a post–Civil War house and filled its six bedrooms with antiques and warm spirit. A little pond sits quietly under your window, and the Tichenors will be delighted to talk to you about local history or their many travels.

Rockingham County

The **Daniel Harrison House,** southwest of Harrisonburg and just north of Dayton, also is known as Fort Harrison. The front part of this sturdy stone structure was built in about 1748, with the rest of the house constructed in the 1850s. When the nonprofit organization formed by the Harrisonburg-Rockingham Historical Society purchased the property in 1978, they started immediate restoration, including dismantling and rebuilding the east and west stone walls. Within the past few years, they have repainted the interior and exterior and redone the floors. Some original cedar shingles were found in the attic and replicated. A group of local archeologists have searched for the hidden tunnel that supposedly connected the house to the nearby spring and that reportedly was used as protection from the marauding Indians. That search has not been completed, and the society hopes to continue it this summer. The house is open from May 16 through October 31, from 1:00 P.M. to 5:00 P.M. and at other times, such as during Dayton Days and around the winter holidays for the craft sale. Tours are available for school groups and others by calling Mary Mullen at (703) 879–9965 or (703) 879–2280. There is no admission charge, but donations are accepted, and the society is always looking for Shenandoah Valley furniture pieces dating prior to 1870.

Shenandoah County

The **Shenandoah Valley Music Festival,** held every summer at Orkney Springs, is one of the outstanding events of its type. Started in 1962, the programs vary from the great masterworks for orchestra to light classical music, lilting pops, vocal music, and Big Band sounds. You could not ask for a more beautiful setting in which to hear beautiful music (and it's mountain informal to boot). William Hudson, director of the Fairfax Symphony, is the artistic director and administrator for the nonprofit festival.

Meals can be reserved at the Orkney Springs Hotel by calling (703) 856–2198, and soft drinks are sold from a festival lawn concession. Of course, you're invited to bring your own picnic to eat on the lawn before the concert. Individual ticket prices range from $1 for children and $8 for adults for lawn seats to $10 for regular pavilion seats and $12.50 for preferred pavilion (more comfortable) seats. A limited number of tickets are sold at the door. Take exit 69 off Interstate 81 and go east on Route 703. Then turn right onto Route 11 through Mt. Jackson and turn right onto Route 263. Follow it (going west) for 15 miles. For more information or discount subscription tickets, write to the Shenandoah Valley Music Festival, P.O. Box 12, Woodstock 22664 or call (703) 459–3396.

Edward (b. 1915) and Maxine Heberlein and their son Ed, Jr., and his wife, Marty, operate the **Tuttle & Spice General Store Museum** in Shenandoah Caverns. They call it the most interesting store in the valley. Edward Heberlein, who says he is a "collector of collections," and Maxine opened the museum in 1976 with collections of mechanical banks, locally handmade brooms, Meerschaum pipes, a railroad layout, and other interesting items.

Now the museum features displays of Munsingwear underwear, a Cottage Arctic Soda apparatus—a drugstore item of Italian marble with eight soda dispensers patented on April 27, 1869—some 1,000 patent medicines, pharmaceuticals, and a Crigler's Orchestrion (nickelodeon) priced at $4,995, all in an 1880s style.

These collections of old-time items are displayed in what has grown to eight different rooms designed to replicate a drugstore, haberdashery, dry goods store, tobacco shop, hardware store, and other typical rooms of the time. These little museums are filled from top to bottom with brass beds, tobacco for chewing, smoking, and snuff, chandeliers, lanterns, corsets, high button shoes, china doll heads, elixirs, and even the storekeeper's booze.

This is a museum for which the word *incredible* comes close to being inadequate. What's even more incredible is that there's no charge for this museum. Under the same roof is an operating General Store, owned by Mrs. Anderson, who sells old-fashioned hard candy, snacks, dolls and dollhouses, and gifts. Take exit 68 off Interstate 81. Their address is Shenandoah Caverns 22847, and their phone number is (703) 477-2601.

The **Strasburg Museum** is housed in an 1891 building originally constructed as a steam pottery. Reportedly the first potter came to Strasburg in 1765, and since then at least seventeen potters have produced earthen- and stoneware here. The building is also a former southern railway depot, and items from the eighteenth and nineteenth centuries are displayed as though they are being used. Strasburg pottery, at one time made in this building, also is exhibited, and there's a quaint country-style gift shop. The museum is open from 10:00 A.M. to 4:00 P.M., May through October, and it's located on King Street just past the Strasburg Hotel. Call (703) 465-3175.

Bob and Peg's Vintage Village features what Bob calls a "working museum dedicated to the preservation of antique and classic motor vehicles. Working museums (where in this case you can watch people working on old cars, rather than just view them in a finished condition) are a thing of the past. Probably about thirty years ago there were a lot of working museums in the country," but there aren't many today. He and Peg have about fifty to seventy-five projects going on all the time, featuring just about any mode of transportaion from biplanes to motorcycles to buggies. They're trying to present a range of cars that you normally wouldn't see in an antique automobile museum.

His museum includes radio-controlled airplanes on stainless steel cables that can be battery or electrically operated and also features little areas depicting a general store, a turn-of-the-century firehouse, a train station, a World War I field hospital, a blacksmith shop, a millinery store, Wilbur and Orville Wright's bicycle shop, a one-room schoolhouse, a western saloon (which soon will be a research library and lunchroom), a jail house, and a hotel. Bob is looking for mannequins, old glasses, items from country schools, old doors and windows, antique toys and bicycles, display cases, and fire company items to buy or borrow.

The museum (703–465–5737) is open daily from 10:00 A.M. to 4:00 P.M. Admission is $3.50 for adults, $.50 for children 12 and over, and free for those under twelve. It's on Route 1 (Box 388) in Strasburg, between exits 73 and 74 on Interstate 81.

If you'd really like to drive through a covered bridge, then head toward the **Meems Bottom Bridge** between Mount Jackson and New Market over the north fork of the Shenandoah River. It was built in 1893 of materials hewed and quarried nearby and was nearly destroyed by fire in 1976. It was reopened in 1979 and then closed again due to structural problems. It has since reopened. Mount Jackson says the bridge is 191 feet long; the Virginia Division of Tourism says it's 204 feet. In any case, it's apparently the longest covered bridge in the state.

This single-span Theodore Burr truss, built under the supervision of F. S. Wisler, succeeded at least two other bridges. Records show that one was burned in 1862 as Jackson went up the valley ahead of Fremont prior to the battles of Harrisonburg. Another was washed away during a flood in 1870. "Up the valley" here is southward, since the river flows northward to join the Potomac at Harpers Ferry.

The bridge is easily reached by taking exit 68 from Interstate 81 to Highway 11 and turning west on Route 720.

Do stop by the Shenandoah Valley Visitor Center, just off Interstate 81 at New Market, and talk with the marvelously friendly and competent staff who will help lead you to your specific interests. Open daily from 9:00 A.M. to 5:00 P.M. Write the Shenandoah Valley Travel Association, P.O. Box 1040, Department CE88, New Market 22844 or call (703) 740–3132.

Warren County

Alpenglow is a carbonated, alcohol-free apple cider bottled in champagne-shaped bottles at the Linden Beverage Company in the Linden area. It's made from Red Delicious and Winesap apples (about a three-to-one ratio) grown in the Lacy family's mountaintop orchards above the Shenandoah Valley. The Lacys say the high altitude and some rare climate conditions produce apples that are "sweeter and more intensely flavored than Valley-grown fruit." Alpenglow has no added sugar and no preservatives.

Take a free taste of the cider and mulled cider as you walk into the **Apple House** country store. Bottles are under $3 a fifth. Also available, usually, are apple pie and apple donuts. Take exit 3 in Linden off Interstate 66 to Route 55 and turn right (away from Linden). The Apple House will be on your right. Or, if you're coming from Front Royal, stay on Route 55 out of Front Royal, and the Apple House will be on your left. It's open from 8:30 A.M. to 6:00 P.M. Call (703) 635–5481 for more details.

Off the Beaten Path in Northern Virginia

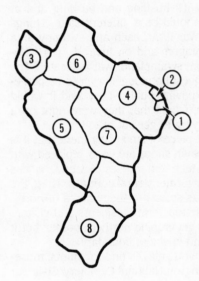

1. Alexandria
   Torpedo Factory
   Farmers Market
   George Washington
   Masonic National
   Memorial
   Mount Vernon Trail
2. Arlington County
   Lyndon Baines Johnson
   Park
   National Inventors Hall of
   Fame
3. Clarke County
   Coiner's Department Store
   Enders Mortuary Museum
   White Post Restorations
   Burwell-Morgan Mill

4. Fairfax County
   Future Farmers of America
   Washington's Grist Mill
   Colvin Run Mill Park
   Lazy Susan Dinner
   Theatre
5. Fauquier County
   Meredyth Vineyards
   Warrenton Soaring Center
6. Loudoun County
   Washington Concorde SST
   Hill High Orchards
   White's Ferry
   American Work Horse
   Museum
7. Prince William County
   Occoquan
   Weems-Botts Museum
   Globe and Laurel
   Restaurant
   Marine Corps Air and
   Ground Museum
   Manassas Museum
   Manassas Battlefield Park
8. Spotsylvania County
   Old Stone Warehouse
   Kenmore
   McGrath House
   Fredericksburg Colonial
   Inn
   Falmouth

Northern Virginia

There was a time when northern Virginia was that little bit of land across the Potomac River. It was filled with pawn shops and other things, and oh, yes, Mount Vernon, where you went for your long Sunday drive. Now it's hustling and bustling and at times must feel as though it should be a different state. Things started changing with World War II. A beach and swampy area were filled in to build the Pentagon, and on June 15, 1941, National Airport (also claimed from swampland) was dedicated. The newspapers said it was the biggest boondoggle ever to be perpetrated upon the American taxpaying public. They said it would never be used to capacity. Oh, would that they were right on a Friday evening when you're trying to get out of town!

Northern Virginia is still that piece of land "over there," but it is also so much more. First, the pawn shops are gone, replaced with high-rise buildings and high-tech enterprises. Second, it has spread to include several other formerly rural counties. Third, the Washington subway system has spread to the suburbs of northern Virginia, and its dozens of stops bring residents and visitors even closer. A river defines its geographic northern border, but it is difficult to define a social and business boundary.

With all this "modern" stuff, you still will find fox hunts, museums, waterfalls, grist mills, Arlington National Cemetery, Civil War battlefields, and claim to history.

Virginia: Off The Beaten Path covers some of the well-known spots but more as jumping-off places than as destinations. Within the figurative shadow of the Washington Monument, we'll explore a mortuary museum (thought to be the only one in the country), uncover an automobile restoration facility where millionaires take their cars to be brought back to life, explore a hiking and biking trail that runs under the flight path of National Airport, investigate an old canal that was vital to the shipping industry not too many distant years ago, enjoy the area's variety of parks, and let your wallet loose in one of the oldest and most unconventional department stores in the country.

Virginia tourism addresses the contradictory nature of northern Virginia by saying it is "where cosmopolitan meets country." It certainly is the place where you can still take your choice.

Alexandria

The Ramsey House Alexandria Welcome Center is the place to start your Alexandria touring. You'll be offered information (including an extensive listing of antique shops) and a pass that allows out-of-town visitors free parking at the regular meters (not the twenty-minute meters). The pass is in the form of an Honorary Citizen of Alexandria proclamation signed by the mayor and Barbara Janney, director of Alexandria's Tourist Council. The certificate is good for seventy-two hours and should be placed on the dashboard, face up, on the *passenger* side of the car. Talk with Diane Bechtol, manager of public relations at the Welcome Center, if you have time, for specific suggestions of what to see and do tailored to your interests. Open 9:00 A.M. to 5:00 P.M., seven days a week except Christmas, Thanksgiving, and New Year's. The Welcome Center is at 221 King Street. Call (703) 838–4200 or (703) 838–5005 (twenty-four–hour recording).

Most of the museums, many of the galleries, and a large number of the artists at the Torpedo Factory (see below) are not open or available on Mondays. That means you can find parking more easily, but you may not be able to visit as much.

Fortunately, almost everything of historic, artistic, and shopping interest in Alexandria is within walking distance (if you park centrally and you're a good walker). The walk from the King Street Metro is a little far and not really practical for most sightseeing or shopping trips (carrying back those purchases).

Along your walk, you can see the narrowest houses in Alexandria in the 400 block of Prince Street and the 500 block of Queen Street. These were alley houses built between two other houses. Sometimes they were called spite houses or mother-in-law houses. Alexandria features a Flounder house architectural style that may be unique. A typical house was cut in half the long way, was usually much taller and narrower than normal, and was probably built to satisfy a provision of the sale of the lots that the property would be improved within two years. People who envisioned building something grander started with the Flounder, which became a minor wing when the larger front part was constructed. The original section usually was built without windows because of taxes on glass or windows.

Alexandria has a new "official" guest house for visiting VIPs. The eighteenth-century house has been decorated by noted designer Frankie Welch and will be used for official guests of the city, meetings, fashion shows, teas, and luncheons. The first floor is home to Frankie's business, which has seen her create designs for Highbee's department store in Indianapolis and Manhattan Motors in suburban Maryland. For your own design, stop by Frankie's shop, 305 Cameron Street, or call (703) 549–0104.

At least two real cobblestone streets still exist, in the 100 block of Prince Street and the 600 block of Princess Street (both residential streets). Legend has it the Hessian prisoners of war laid the cobblestone, which had been ballast in the ships coming across the Atlantic. Along the waterfront you'll see the Captain's Row, where the sea captains used to live. Offices were downstairs and living premises were upstairs. The 200 block of Prince Street, known as Gentry Row, is noted for the size and elegance of the houses. Although these are private residences, many are open during a variety of "weeks" such as Garden Week and Christmas Walk, so check the calendar at the Welcome Center if you'd like to see these magnificent properties. Guided walking tours led by a costumed guide are available through the Welcome Center on Monday and Saturday in the spring and fall, or by appointment, for a small charge.

One of the most widely imitated art forms is the transformation of the **Torpedo Factory** (a 1918 factory where torpedo shell cases were built) into a facility now housing more than 200 artists in three floors of studio space. You can buy original artworks (weaving, paintings, musical instruments, pots, prints, sculptures, jewelry, glassworks, and photography) after you've talked with the artist, attend lectures, take art classes, and take part in a variety of other activities. The city's Urban Archeology Museum and research lab is located on the third floor (open 11:00 A.M. to 5:00 P.M. Friday and Saturday). You can also see an MK-14 torpedo on display on the first floor.

The Torpedo Factory, 105 North Union Street, is open from 10:00 A.M. to 5:00 P.M. daily; the phone number is (703) 838–4565.

On the river side of the Torpedo Factory is the new waterfront area, the scene of much water-related activity. The *New Zealand,* the yacht that lost to *Stars and Stripes* in the 1988 America's Cup race and was later declared the winner when a New York superior court ruled that the United States had sailed an illegal boat (a catamaran), stopped by the Torpedo Factory marina and was open for tours. The *Spirit of Massachusetts* brought in some blustery Boston winds for an open house. The *Gazela,* one of the Class A Tall Ships, attended the six-block-long Alexandria Red Cross Waterfront Festival.

The Swedish-built three-masted topsail schooner *Alexandria* honors the city that was once the third largest port in the country, and is used for sailing education as a four-man crew navigates the schooner to port cities where tourists can learn about the ship's heritage. In 1988 it underwent $150,000 worth of repairs at the Norfolk shipyard. She placed second in the 1980 Tall Ships Race and escorted the Christian Radich, a Norwegian training vessel, in the 1986 Statue of Liberty Parade of Sails. The schooner was constructed in 1929, and is 92 feet at deck level with an overall length of 125 feet and spreads more than 7000 square feet of red sails. It's said she's built like a fortress with three-inch oak planking on 8-inch double-sawn oak frames.

Adults who are interested in maritime history who would like to become volunteer tour guides are welcome. Call the Alexandria Seaport Foundation. The *Alexandria* is open to the public on weekends from noon to 5:00 P.M. when she's in port. Call (703) 549–7078.

To discover the importance of the waterfront to Alexandria's history, stop by the Alexandria Waterfront Museum, part of the city's Office of Historic Alexandria. It overlooks the restored tidal lock of the Alexandria Canal, which was in operation between 1843 and 1886. The first exhibit was about trade and prosperity and recounted the history of the canal. This was an easy way for boats to travel from the C & O Canal in Georgetown, across the Potomac River, while avoiding the shallow water of the river, by means of the Aqueduct Bridge, just north of Key Bridge. A photo shows a canal barge crossing the Potomac. The lock was uncovered in 1978 and was in very good condition, despite having been under tons of topsoil all these years. Several pictures by Matthew Brady show the lock and the local wharf. A video and exhibit fill in the details. The museum is at 44 Canal Center Plaza in the TransPotomac Canal Center and is open Tuesday through Friday, 11:00 A.M. to 4:00 P.M. and 1:00 P.M. to 4:00 P.M. weekends. Admission is free, but donations are gladly accepted.

About a block north of the museum is a sculpture garden with an interplay of a lot of pieces that are actually only one piece; the setting of water and sculpture produces an interesting look.

The Alexandria **Farmers Market,** on the south plaza of City Hall at 301 King Street, was established in the original lot sale of

July 1749, when two lots were designated for the purpose. The farmers market started in 1753 and is said to be the nation's oldest continuously operating market. George Washington, born near Fredericksburg, spent his young adult life in this area and is said to have sent produce here to be sold. The market moves indoors during the winter to the lobby of City Hall. Farmers come early, about 5:30 A.M., as do wise shoppers. You may see notices that it's open until 9:30 A.M., but your selections will be slim, if any. Call (703) 838-4770.

Hearthstone Bookshop, at 8405-H Richmond Highway, is billed as the "Genealogy Store," the only bookstore on the East Coast specializing in genealogy, local history, and Americana. They say they have everything you need to trace your family tree, including books, periodicals, maps, charts, forms, and accessories, with aids to research such ethnic groups as English, Irish, Scottish, French, German, Scandinavian, and central European. It's open from 10:00 A.M. to 5:00 P.M. Monday through Saturday and noon to 5:00 P.M. on Sunday. Their phone number is (703) 360-6900.

The most visible sight in Alexandria, the **George Washington Masonic National Memorial,** also provides the most spectacular view of the city and of Washington, D.C., 6 miles away. You'll want to bring your widest and longest camera lenses to shoot from the observation tower of this 333-foot building. The main lobby features two 46-by-18-foot murals by Allyn Cox, one depicting the laying of the cornerstone of the United States Capitol in September 1793 and one of General Washington at a religious service on St. John's Day 1778, in Christ Church, Philadelphia. There's a 17-foot-3-inch bronze statue of George Washington in the Memorial Hall and a collection of Washington memorabilia, including the clock that was stopped when he died. The auditorium is surrounded by granite columns and bronze medallions of the U.S. presidents who have been Freemasons. The Parade Room contains an elaborate display of a mechanical parade of miniature uniformed Shrine Units.

The Shrine Rooms East (703-683-2007) are open daily (except holidays) from 9:00 A.M. to 5:00 P.M., and there is no admission charge. Scheduled tower tours are held periodically from 9:15 A.M. through 4:00 P.M. There's plenty of free parking, and it's also within walking distance (uphill) of the King Street Metro station. Although not accessible to the handicapped, Masonic Brothers visiting the Shrine will be helped by other Brothers. The memorial is atop Shooters Hill at the west end of King Street.

Still another viewpoint of the area is along the **Mount Vernon Trail,** which parallels the George Washington Memorial Parkway from Mount Vernon to north of Alexandria. Starting south at the Arlington Memorial Bridge (dedicated in 1932 to symbolize the union of the North and South following the Civil War), you go past the Lyndon Baines Johnson Memorial Grove in Lady Bird Johnson Park, the Navy-Marine Memorial (the Ernesto Begni del Piatta statue honoring Americans who served at sea, dedicated in 1934), Gravelly Point, which is a terrific place to view the takeoffs and landings at National Airport, Old Town Alexandria, Jones Point Lighthouse (in service from 1836 to 1925) and Dyke Marsh (a 240-acre wetland where over 250 species of birds have been sighted), catch a look at Fort Washington (on the Maryland side) and end at Mount Vernon.

You can walk, jog or bike the length of this 17-mile trail or just parts of it. There are at least two or three places in Alexandria where you can rent a bike for an hour or a day. Check with the Welcome Center for more information. Three areas are quite steep and might be a little strenuous for new bikers. There are plenty of places to picnic and to enjoy nature and history, and a physical fitness course helps you vary the type of exercise you're doing. Call (703) 426–6600 for more information. In 1988, a new section of trail opened to link the Custis-Lee, Interstate 66 Trail, and the Mount Vernon Trail. This 1.5-mile-long connection enables cyclists and others to travel on a continuous developed trail that runs 64 miles between Mount Vernon and Purcellville.

You can take a variety of daylong excursions and one-way ferry trips over many lines of the Norfolk Southern Railroad, successor to the Southern and Norfolk and Western railroads. Almost every trip is sponsored by on-line chapters of the National Railway Historical Society, railway museums, or railroad and civic clubs. Two steam trains operate simultaneously, and the trains are air-conditioned and have open-window coaches, commissary cars, and specially built open-sided observation cars. Some of the trips might include Norfolk to Petersburg, Roanoke to Lynchburg, and Alexandria to Charlottesville.

The main offices are located at 12121 Eisenhower in Alexandria and you can write to them at P.O. Box 19869, Alexandria 22320–0869 or talk with James A. Bistline, general manager of steam operations, at (703) 684–4399. You can also write to the local clubs listed below about the year's schedule of upcoming trips: Old Dominion Chapter (ODC), P.O. Box 8583, Richmond 23226;

Roanoke Chapter (RCN), P.O. Box 13222, Roanoke 24032; Virginia Museum of Transportation, 802 Wiley Dr., S.W., Roanoke 24015; Tidewater Chapter (TWC), P.O. Box 7185, Portsmouth 23707.

Arlington County

If you stop by the seventeen-acre **Lyndon Baines Johnson Park** mentioned above in connection with the Mount Vernon Trail, you will find white pine, dogwoods, numerous flowering bushes, and a tape recording of Lady Bird Johnson's remarks at the dedication ceremony in 1976. They are played through an outdoor speaker installed at one end of the footbridge that connects the grove to the Pentagon parking lot. There is also a forty-three-ton obelisk that was brought in from the Marble Falls Quarry, near the LBJ Ranch in Johnson City, Texas. If it looks rough, that's because it has been sculpted to give it a rugged look.

There are no quotations or citations proclaiming Johnson's victories while in office. There are just peace and tranquility and natural beauty signifying the Johnsons' contributions to our national park system and the highway beautification program.

Millions upon millions of patents are kept on file in the Patent and Trademark Office at Crystal City. You can research an idea or the history of an invention there, but you can also visit the **National Inventors Hall of Fame** and possibly attend the festivities on National Inventors Day, held on a weekend near February 11, the birthday of Thomas A. Edison, the first Hall of Fame inductee. Edison's patent for the electric lamp was No. 223,898, and it was one of 1,093 patents he received. Also honored are Alexander Graham Bell, Eli Whitney, Samuel Morse, the Wright Brothers, Charles Goodyear, Cyrus McCormick, George Eastman, Edwin Herbert Land, Louis Pasteur, Robert Hutchings Goddard and many, many others. Recent inductees are Frank B. Colton, for the discovery of oral contraceptives; Elisha Graves Otis, inventor of an elevator safety mechanism (which allowed skyscrapers to be constructed); Louis W. Parker, inventor of the television receiver; and An Wang, who discovered the magnetic pulse controlling device, the principle upon which computer memory is based.

The Hall of Fame is in the lobby of 2021 Jeff Davis Highway and is open from 8:00 A.M. to 8:00 P.M. Monday through Friday. You can take the metro system to the Crystal City section and walk south about three blocks to Crystal Plaza Number 3 Building. Call (703) 557–3341 for more details.

In 1940, Auriel Bessemer painted seven scenes entitled *Historical and Industrial Scenes and Sketches of Virginia* as WPA murals in the Arlington Post Office, showing beginning settlements with native Americans up to 1940. The post office is at 3118 North Washington Street.

Clarke County

Like a one-man, self-propelled whirlwind, Billy Thompson promotes the pleasures of Clarke County and all else that is dear to its residents. Billy says, "There are no skyscrapers or amusement parks, but what we do have is a lot of beauty—it's always there—and a tremendous amount of historic points of interest, and people from the city come out here for that purpose. They don't come here for the amusement park." People do come, generally from within 200 miles, but also from a far as Ontario, Canada. Clarke County celebrated its sesquicentennial in 1986 with a series of events Thompson and 150 other people worked on for two years.

Through the Berryville–Clarke County Chamber of Commerce, he'll conduct half-day or two-day tours that will take you to beautiful little waterfalls or on a 10-mile trip through three or four different horse farms (don't expect to see horses out in the fields during the summer days, for it's too hot, and they won't be put out in the pastures until later in the day). You may stop by a training farm and therapeutic center where you'll see an indoor swimming pool and whirlpool for the horses, or see where they keep 200 hounds for fox hunting. The dairy farm gives free ice cream and milk. You may see an apple or tomato produce-packing operation such as the one at Shady Grove. On other trips, Billy will show Bears Den, a big rock on the edge of a mountain, where on a clear day you can see as far as you want to see. You might sit where George Washington sat and ate his lunch while he was surveying the area.

The tours are for groups and must be arranged ahead of time. There's a nominal charge that goes to the Chamber of Commerce, plus any food you purchase and the admission charge if you go into Burwell-Morgan Mill. Check with Billy to see if there's a group you can join. The Berryville–Clarke County Chamber of Commerce is at 105 North Church Street in Berryville; (703) 955–4200.

A Berryville walking tour map is available that will lead you by sixteen points of interest, from the Berryville Presbyterian Church, where services were conducted as early as 1737, to the Main Street Barber Shop, with its stepped wooden parapet, interior chimney, and recessed entrance (said once to have been used as a jail). Pick up a map at Berryville–Clarke County Chamber of Commerce.

In Berryville, the county seat, you'll find a historical museum at the Old Courthouse, built in 1739. It's open by appointment, and the artifacts are changed every three months. Check with the Chamber.

Coiner's Department Store at 24 East Main Street, established in 1896, advertised and advertises "everything for everybody." Two brothers, E. G. and Victor, opened the store with an argument over whether it would be spelled Coiner or Coyner, a reflection of the way each brother spelled his last name. They settled on Coyner and Coiner's until 1913, when E. G. became the sole owner and it became Coiner's. Chester Hobert of Ohio, a traveling salesman for Bingham Hardware Company, sold merchandise to Mr. Coiner beginning in 1927, at the age of 24. When Mr. Coiner retired in 1946, he sold the store to Hobert, who still runs the store, although he now has help from his son Michael and Michael's wife.

The original "cash carrier" system, looking much like a fleet of cable cars, takes the money and sales slips to the office via pulleys and sends the carrier with change back to the customer via gravity. There are no cash registers in Coiner's. Another relic is the still-used pulley-operated freight elevator, built in Baltimore, Maryland. It's had two major breakdowns recently, and repair is a serious problem, for there are few people left who know about the old elevators, and fewer know how to fix them.

Michael has made some modern merchandising changes but says this type of department store isn't long for the world. It won't be from the competition of discount stores or big chains but from the death of the tradition of the traveling salesman who carried many, many different lines of merchandise. You're invited to Coiner's Department Store to inspect the carpentry work done by the original owners and other interesting features of this living museum.

The post office on Church Street features a 1938 WPA mural of a horse country and livestock farm entitled *Clarke County Prod-*

ucts, 1939 by local painter Edwin S. "Ned" Lewis, who specialized in horse paintings and local scenes (see his WPA painting in the Petersburg Post Office). The locals will tell you Mr. Lewis painted this mural as a contribution to the post office, which may explain why it's dated 1938 but wasn't officially completed until 1940.

Of all the museums we heard about and visited, perhaps the **Enders Mortuary Museum** at 101 East Main Street in Berryville will classify as the most unusual. The Enders Funeral Home, started by John Enders in 1892, is one of the oldest continously operating businesses in the county and still the only mortuary in Clarke County. They had the first telephone in Berryville and started the fire company. Reggie Shirley, who took over the funeral home in the early 1970s, started the museum in 1983 after searching through the attic and finding turn-of-the-century documents and implements of funeral days gone by. The museum shows old caskets, documents, embalming implements, cosmetic jars, and a horse-drawn hearse from 1889 (restored by White Post Restorations). Hours are 9:00 A.M. to 5:00 P.M. Monday through Friday and 9:00 A.M. to noon on Saturday. The museum is closed during services. Call (703) 955–1062 for information.

As you continue south on Route 340 from Berryville, you reach a fork in the road where a green water pump and a small park mark the place to turn off for White Post. Billy Thompson says there are about 200 souls in White Post, the same as when it was surveyed originally. The town has a real whitewashed post originally set there by George Washington when he surveyed in 1750. People used to run into the post, but it hasn't been hit in twenty years since the main road bypassed the town. It's a big locust post that will do more damage to a car than the auto will do to the post.

Billy Thompson operates out of **White Post Restorations** in White Post. He was born in the house in front of the shop. When he was two years old his father built a four-bay shop. Back in 1958 Billy knew he had to expand and specialize, so he started restoring antique cars. Not only do they work on old cars, but they also run a museum that you can visit at no charge. Inside are old signs, Virginia license plates going back to 1910 (including one that isn't even dated, a cardboard license plate from 1944, and an aluminum plate from 1947), toy trucks, and lots of beautiful classic cars (they have a front wheel Cord, a 1926 Buick, and a Model-T) that have been restored or are in the process of restora-

White Post

tion from the very frame up. About 100 cars a year go through the shop. Billy figures these cars have about 50,000 pieces each. His shop takes them apart completely, logging each and every part and reconstructing pieces if necessary in one of his seven departments (woodworking, mechanical, upholstery, metalcrafting, etc.). Call (703) 837–1140 for information.

The bread from the Abbey of the Holy Cross Monastery is legendary. (Safeway and Giant grocery stores carry the baked goods, preservative free and made from unbleached and stone-ground flours, spring water, and unsulfured molasses.) The monastery is on the site of the historic Wormley Estate, a well-preserved, 200-year-old stone building. You're invited to stop by, but call first. It's on Route 2 in Berryville; call (703) 955–3933.

If you don't go on one of Billy's tours, you still can visit the **Burwell-Morgan Mill** in Millwood. It's an operating overshot waterwheel with wooden gears dating from 1750, built of stone by former Hessian soldiers captured at the Battle of Saratoga, and clapboard, which was added in 1876. Lt. Col. Nathaniel Burwell and Brig. Gen. Daniel Morgan started the operation in 1782, and during the Civil War flour and feed from the mill were sold to both armies. It was an unusual mill in that the abundant water supply and huge 20-foot-diameter wheel achieved 45 horsepower, compared to an average of only 20 horsepower. The mill remained in operation until 1953. It's open May through October, Wednesday through Monday from 9:30 A.M. to 4:30 P.M. Admission is $1 for adults and $.50 for children. Millwood is located on Route 723, off Highway 50 before Route 255. (703) 837–1799.

Fairfax County

Three miles down the road from Mount Vernon is the home of the **Future Farmers of America.** In its basement is a farm museum and a farming National Hall of Achievement. Farmers and farms have been of increasing interest lately, and it might take the flow chart on the museum wall to bring the issue into focus. The chart traces the decrease in the number of farmers from 1928, when there were 32,000,000 farmers and 6,000,000 farms, to mid-1972, when there were 10,000,000 farmers and 3,000,000 farms. Also interesting is the increasing number of students in agriculture studies, a number that has grown considerably over the years. Membership in FFA, however, has been decreasing, which might be a further sign of our farming trends. As of July 1985, Virginia had 14,704 FFA members, down more than a thousand from 1984, which was down more than a thousand from 1983.

Museum hours are 8:00 A.M. to 4:30 P.M., Monday through Friday, and tours of the entire FFA Center are available by appointment. The FFA (703–360–3600) is at 5632 Mount Vernon Highway, just before it intersects with Highway 1 and Highway 235.

Almost next to the FFA offices is **Washington's Grist Mill,** a reconstruction of Washington's 1772 stone mill on Dogue Creek when the creek was still navigable. The mill was three and one-half stories high with an interior wheel. During the careful excavation, part of the wheel, bearings for the wheel, part of the trundlehead, complete wheel buckets, and other items were found. Conducted tours of the mill are available. The mill is at 5514 Mount Vernon Memorial Highway (703–780–3383).

Colvin Run Mill Park is barely outside the hustle and bustle of the ever-growing Tysons Corner area. Yet, you can spend an afternoon learning how to carve small wood animals and talking with Sue Baker or any of the 400 members of the Northern Virginia Wood Carvers. Or, you can watch the restored, early nineteenth-century mill in operation, tour a miller's house (both built by Philip Carper), walk through a dairy barn, buy items from the general store, or just have a family outing. You can also have an office party, a country wedding, or a candlelit supper. Colvin Run Mill Park is located off Leesburg Pike (Route 7) at 10017 Colvin Run Road in Great Falls, miles west of Tysons. Phone numbers are (703) 534–1845 (woodcarvers) or (703) 759–2771 (park).

Fauquier County

Virginia has been growing in significance as a wine-growing area over the past decade, and one of the vineyards that features award-winning estate bottled wines, tours, and other activities is **Meredyth Vineyards** outside of Middleburg. Here you might find a mystery outing combined with wine tasting, an Appalachian music and dance evening (box supper catered by the Red Fox), Renaissance and baroque music, Ed Steel of Middletown's

Colvin Run Mill Park

Wayside Theater as Mark Twain, or a chance to view some of the wildlife, including rabbits, groundhogs, whitetail deer, red fox or even a turtle. Take time to meet Archie M. Smith, president, or write to him at P.O. Box 347, Middleburg, VA 22117 to be placed on the mailing list.

There's no charge to tour for small groups, but large groups are $1 per person, by appointment. Hours are daily 10:00 A.M. to 4:00 P.M., except Christmas, Easter, Thanksgiving, and New Year's Day. From Middleburg go west on Highway 50, take a left at the flashing yellow light at Madison Street, go 2 1/2 miles, turn right onto Route 628 for another 2 1/2 miles, and the entrance to Meredyth will be on your right. Call (703) 687-6277 or 478-1835 from Washington.

Most of us love to get into the air for the splendid feeling of freedom, and the **Warrenton Soaring Center** is the place to go. The view of Virginia's famous hunt country and out toward the foothills of the Blue Ridge Mountains is spectacular. Facilities and equipment are available for those who own gliders, qualified glider pilots, and power pilots who want to learn gliding. If you've never flown in a glider, you can take lessons. From the first time out you will fly the glider yourself (an instructor will be with you). After straight flight and gentle turns you'll get into takeoffs, tow, and landings, and then you solo. After instruction, solo flights, flight time, and examination, you'll be ready to take your friends soaring.

The center is open on weekends (weather permitting) from 9:00 A.M. to 5:00 P.M. Warrenton Soaring Center can be reached by taking the exit to Gainsville off Interstate 66; go south on Route 29 for 3 1/2 miles, past the Warrenton bypass, then turn left at Route 616. The Warrenton Airpark is 1 1/2 miles on the right. Call (703) 347-0054.

For those who long for the good ole days, but don't want to go back quite as far as the Civil or Revolutionary wars, the Flying Circus Aerodrome near Bealeton relives the days of the daring young men in their flying machines as the circus goes barnstorming over the countryside every Sunday from 2:30 P.M. to 4:00 P.M., May through October. You'll see wing walking, precision aerobatics, hot-air ballooning, skydiving, and comedy, and you'll hold your breath all the while. Bring a picnic basket for late lunch or early dinner. Admission is $5 for adults and $2 for children three to twelve. From Interstate 95, take Route 17 west to Route

644, near Bealeton, turn right and follow the signs. (703) 439-8661.

Loudoun County

It's not every day you have a chance to see the **Concorde SST,** but at Washington's Dulles International Airport you can see the British Airways Concorde every day except Monday. It lands and takes off between noon and 1:00 P.M. (times are approximate). You cannot board, but you can go to the observation deck to watch.

One-hour tours of the airport are available and can be tailored to specific interests, like architecture, and to special guests, like international visitors and senior citizens (everything's accessible). They generally include a fifteen-minute film, a walk through the terminal building, a ride on a mobile lounge, and, if there are fewer than twenty in the group and the visitors are at least fourth or fifth graders and above, a visit to the fire department.

For reservations to tour the airport call Cathy Thomas, assistant to the airport manager, preferably several weeks in advance (703-471-7838). Cathy will take groups from ten to about fifty or sixty people (all at least kindergarten age) at 10:00 A.M. Monday through Friday. Singles or families can call and try to join an organized group scheduled to tour. Buses can park in the bus parking lot, individual cars in the daily lot. Take the Dulles access road (not the toll road) to the airport from the beltway (Interstate 495) or from any of the accesses along the route.

As you're climbing out of Leesburg on Route 7 you'll see John Sleeter's **Hill High Orchards,** one of the many places in this area where you can pick your own strawberries (May 25 through June 15), vegetables, and tree fruit. The orchard is 1 mile east of Round Hill (look for the large yellow arrow), and a retail store with jelly, honey, cider, fresh-baked pies, and bedding plants is 1 mile west of Round Hill (look for the covered wagon). The store is open daily from June to October, 8:00 A.M. to 7:00 P.M., and from November to May, 8:00 A.M. to 5:30 P.M. Call before planning to come out to pick (703-338-7997, or 471-1448 from the Washington area).

Since 1833, ferry boats have been moving travelers across the Potomac River between **White's Ferry** (on the Maryland side) and the Leesburg, Virginia area. It used to be known as Conrad's ferry, but after the Civil War a Confederate officer, Col. Elija V. White, bought and renamed it. It's the only car ferry across the Potomac. For three decades the *Jubal Early* (named for a Confederate general) carried about six cars a trip, but the demand has become so heavy in recent years that owner Malcom Brown installed a new 30-ton vessel in mid-1988 which can carry as many as fifteen cars. The ferry is propelled by a small diesel boat on the upriver side. When it reaches the far side, the ferry pilot casts off a line, and the current carries the small boat around to point it in the right direction for the return trip. The charge is $2.25 for cars, one-way, or $4.00 round-trip (50¢ for pedestrians), and the ferry operates on call from 6:00 A.M. to 8:00 P.M. daily (to 11:00 P.M. in the summer). Take Route 15 north out of Leesburg to the signs.

As Loudoun tries to stay rural and "unsuburban," there are some who acknowledge the fight may already be lost. Dr. Henry Buckardt is working to preserve the lifestyles of years ago. His **American Work Horse Museum,** in Paeonian Springs, was established in 1971 to commemorate the role of the workhorse in American history. A collection of eleven outbuildings sit on the thirty-nine grand acres. Buckhardt's office and library, a black-smith shop, a harness shop, a veterinary building, and a country summer kitchen (where the cooking was done in the summer-time so the main house would stay cool) are among the attractions. But the biggest draw are Sam and Doc, the Clydesdale horses that give life to the static displays (and all look forward to carrot-feeding time). Buckhardt will take you through the build-ings, carefully explaining the use and root of every item. Gen. George C. Marshall and Tom Byrd (of the Virginia Byrds) origi-nally owned and used the garden plows. The museum is open Wednesday, April through October, and by appointment. There's no admission charge. Take Route 7 west to Route 9, then turn left onto Route 662. Call (703) 338–6290 for more information.

Prince William County

Occoquan, an Indian word meaning "at the end of the water," features more than ninety shops (the number has been growing rapidly) and about a half-dozen restaurants in a four-block his-toric square. Many of the shops are working galleries, and others tell their stories through example, as the Country Kitchen at 404 Mill Street, with its construction without nails; Brown's Wood Stuff/The Corner Shop, 403 Mill Street, a former movie house with a raked floor; the Basket Case at 304 Mill Street, a former post office where a hollow was worn in the floor at the service window. For those who enjoy dollhouse miniatures, stop by Bob and Jean Porter's Mountain Valley Miniatures, where you might even find a miniature crab feast complete with crab hammers, spices, and beer. Bob has taught courses in miniature art at the Smithsonian museum in Washington. Fibertique, 406 Mill Street, is thought to be the oldest house in Occoquan. This structure was built in 1742 and is believed to have a ghostly female resident. Another ghost is said to visit the Country Shop, 302 Mill Street, after business hours. Take the walking tour for a complete view of this quaint town. There are no parking meters in Occoquan.

Dumfries, another Scot-settled town, was once a major seaport. Now, pure white whistling swans (perhaps as many as 200) return from Canada to Quantico Creek each year as early as mid-October and leave within twenty-four hours of March 19 (the same date as the Capistrano swallows out west). You can tell when they're getting ready to leave, for they gather in from the various creeks and get very noisy talking things over, and then they all take off at one time.

Just west of Quantico Creek is the **Weems-Botts Museum** at 300 Duke Street, a four-room colonial restoration. One half of the house was once the bookstore of Parson Mason Locke Weems, the biographer of George Washington (*Life of Washington*) who created the legend of the cherry tree. The museum docent tells many little-known facts about George. The museum is open 10:00 A.M. to 5:00 P.M. Monday through Saturday and 1:00 P.M. to 5:00 P.M. on Sunday. No admission charge. Call (703) 221–3346 or (703) 221–3309.

Jumping geographical ground for just a moment, you can browse through a 1962 version of Mason Locke Weem's book, with editorial comments by Marcus Cunliffe, in the Prince William Central Library's Ruth E. Lloyd History Room, Virginiana collection, 8601 Mathis Avenue. Other anecdotal incidents are discussed in the book, such as the story of Washington throwing a stone across the Rappahannock River at the lower ferry of Fredericksburg (which became an even wilder anecdote that had Washington throwing a silver dollar across the much wider Potomac River outside of Washington, D.C.), as well as the history of the book, which started as a pamphlet and grew to 162 pages published in numerous editions over a number of years. Librarian Don Wilson can help you with your historical search or with the nice genealogy section which will be growing when the library moves to its new location on Sudley Road in a few years.

The **Globe and Laurel Restaurant** was opened in old-town Quantico in 1968 by Richard (Major, U.S. Marine Corps, Ret.) and Gloria Spooner, but it burned, and the restaurant was reopened in its new location on Jeff Davis Highway in 1975. Major Spooner was in the Marines for twenty-nine years and seven months and wanted a place with a pub atmosphere. Music of the swing bands or bagpipes fills the air as you dine. Of historic note are the hundreds, maybe thousands, of police department badges on the ceiling from police forces across the country and from about thirty countries. Also of interest is the collection of former military insignia, many of which aren't in the possession of the military historians, for apparently no one thought to save them. He has them going back to the Civil War, and if you have military buttons or other memorabilia, check with Spooner before you throw them away. And while you're at the restaurant, you should try the prime rib. It's quite tasty. The Globe and Laurel is at 18418 Jeff Davis Highway in Triangle (703–221–9825).

All seven blocks of Quantico constitute the only town in the United States completely surrounded by the U.S. Marine Corps; the only land access is through the Quantico Marine Base. For years the town's been totally landlocked, but recently the government deeded four and a half acres of waterfront property to Quantico to build a park, so now it can be reached by the Potomac River as well. The town has its own mayor, five council members, and its own police department. As an indication of the cooperation between the base and the town, Quantico is the only place in the world where Marines are allowed to wear their "utilities" (work uniforms) off base.

At the **Marine Corps Air and Ground Museum** in Quantico aircraft and support equipment tell the history of Marine Corps aviation. The displays are located in two 1920s hangars at the Marine Corps Development and Education Command, so the buildings themselves are historic. The Marine Corps air-ground team was the world's first combining of the traditional ground combat arms with the newly developed flying machines. On display are a Goodyear Corsair, a flight simulator, a Mitsubishi Zero, and one of only two Grumman Wildcats in the United States, and dioramas made by students of Gilbert Junior High School in Gilbert, Arizona, under the direction of Glen Frakes. There's also a small exhibit about the Marines in the movies, with stills and posters from the last forty years of moviemaking. What's really strange about this museum is finding it among all the Revolutionary and Civil War historical markers and parks throughout the state.

The museum is open April 1 to November 28, from 10:00 A.M. to 5:00 P.M. on Tuesday through Sunday and most holidays, including those that fall on Mondays; the museum is closed on all other Mondays and on Easter and Thanksgiving. A research facility is available for those who want to study the collections more intensively. Take the Quantico exit off Interstate 95 and follow the signs after checking in with the gate guard. For more information, call (703) 640–2606.

The **Manassas Museum** is set in a Victorian Romanesque 1896 building (the community's first national bank), where you can see how gristmills spurred the region's development and why two of the Civil War's most famous battles were fought nearby. Collections include period photographs from the Civil War, children's toys of a century ago, and a major exhibit about the 1911 Peace Jubilee, which celebrated the fiftieth anniversary of the battle at Manassas. It's open Tuesday through Saturday, 10:00 A.M. to 5:00 P.M. and is at 9406 Main Street; (703) 368–1873.

The Manassas Walking Tour, which you can take at your leisure, covers the Museum, the 1875 Presbyterian Church, the world's first military railroad, Rohr's Museum (antique cars and a collection of antique toys, dolls, hats, and music boxes), the defenses of Manassas and the Railroad Depot, the Candy Factory, Conner Opera House, and the Old City Hall. A brochure is available for this tour and the driving tour, which warns about the possible lack of parking at the markers and the heavy traffic. Take Route 234 south of Interstate 66.

Manassas was the site of the first and second battles of Manassas, and many of the events are marked in the **Manassas Battlefield Park** (north of Interstate 66 in Manassas), although highway markers have not yet been posted. To assist your historical tour, pick up a *Prince William County Historical Marker Guide* at the welcome center or some of the museums. This will be a nice companion to Margaret T. Peters's *Guidebook to Virginia's Historical Markers,* published for the Virginia Landmarks Commission by the University Press of Virginia, Charlottesville.

Spotsylvania County

Fredericksburg boasts that "George Washington slept in a lot of places, but he lived here." With 350 original buildings built before 1870, the area is steeped in history from colonial times and the Revolutionary and Civil wars. It's possible to stay here several days without seeing everything. Be sure to get your free all-day parking pass at the Fredericksburg Visitor Center, see the audiovisual display, and obtain directions and operating hours for museums, the national parks, and other attractions. A block tour ticket provides a 30 percent discount for admissions to Kenmore, Mary Washington House, Rising Sun Tavern, Hugh Mercer Apothecary Shop, Belmont, and the James Monroe Museum. It's available at the visitors center for $8.50 or at any of these homes. The visitors center (703–373–1776) is at 706 Caroline Street.

The tobacco-leaf–topped lamps in the historic area are not that old. They were erected since 1980 and reflect Fredericksburg's part in the tobacco industry, as it was the central licensing point for tobacco inspection for some years. Fredericksburg is home to Mary Washington College, so you can feel a historic or a more modern tone depending on where you travel. There are dozens of historic and interesting sights to see, particularly in the city's forty-block National Historic District, so we've selected a handful that don't normally seem to draw too much attention.

The Old Stone Warehouse was built of stone and massive wooden beams and once stood four stories tall. It's thought to be the earliest masonry building in the city. The warehouse backs up to the Rappahannock River. This part of the Rappahannock was navigable with a draw of about 12 feet; it's now about 10 feet of silt and a couple of feet of river. With the constant flooding of the Rappahannock, siltation, and the rebuilding and realignment of the Chatham Bridge in the 1930s, the original third level is now level with Sophia Street. The late Roy Butler, an archaeologist, and others have worked on digs in the basement (originally open for warehouse loading at river level) and uncovered years of artifacts, many of which are on display. The dig is open to the public (slight charge), and amateur archaeologists are always welcome (no charge) in for the dig, particularly at another site a mile up the road at Falmouth. They've dug into five different foundations up there, going down to Indian sites. The museum is at 927 Sophia Street, Fredericksburg; (703) 373-1674.

While in the historic area, you'll note about forty antique stores and a few "malls" of antiques in about a four-block area. Pick up a brochure at the visitors center for specialty listings.

Kenmore, a mid-Georgian structure, was built in 1752 by Col. Fielding Lewis for his second wife, Betty, only sister of George Washington. Kenmore contains the finest ornamental plaster-work in America and authentic (but not original) furnishings of the period from the original inventory lists. (Lewis was providing munitions for the war and not receiving payment, and eventually the furnishings had to be auctioned.)

You'll love the hot fresh gingerbread Carla makes (from Mary Washington's original recipe, which you can purchase in the gift shop) and tea in the kitchen or on the lawn. Stroll through the boxwood gardens, restored by the Garden Club of Virginia. There's a marvelous 9-foot 6-inch by 6-foot Daniel Hadley diorama of Colonial Fredericksburg, done in cooperation with the Hagley Museum in Delaware. If you've been taking your walking tour, been to the Stone House, and paid attention to all the de-tails, you'll realize there are some errors in the depiction, such as the height of Sophia Street compared to the river, and the Baptist Church is the newer one, not the older one, but this is such a magnificent diorama that it shouldn't be missed. The Lewis family tree is on display, filling a matrix twenty-nine squares across and forty-nine squares down.

Besides being known for some of the most beautiful rooms in the country, Kenmore is cited as one of the first victories in the fight against suburban development; in 1922 a developer bought Kenmore and planned to demolish the house or convert it into apartments and subdivide the remaining two acres of land.

Kenmore (1201 Washington Street, 703-373-3381) is open seven days a week, from 9:00 A.M. to 5:00 P.M. March through November and 10:00 A.M. to 4:00 P.M. December through February. It's closed December 24, 25, and 31 and January 1. Admission is $4 for adults and $2 for children.

McGrath House, 225 Princess Anne Street, is a bed and

breakfast in a carefully restored house dating from the first quarter of the nineteenth century. Sylvia McGrath offers a choice of three bedrooms with one shared bathroom to the traveler who enjoys a friendly stay in a historic home in the oldest part of Fredericksburg. Enjoy a continental breakfast in the country kitchen, constructed with hand-hewn beams and a brick floor and overlooking a small colonial herb garden (in season). Or, in the evening dusk, share a drink with Sylvia by the fire before retiring to your home. No smoking; pets are allowed sometimes. Call (703) 371–4363.

The **Fredericksburg Colonial Inn,** at 1707 Princess Anne Street, is a pleasant mix of slightly old and new (it was built in the 1920s, and restoration started in 1980), with a rocking chair and player piano in the lobby and quiltlike coverlets and antiques as well as color televisions, refrigerators, and clock radios in each room. The inn's motto is "George didn't sleep here!!! . . . but you can." Talk with Jim Hirst or Patsy Nunnally for the best advice on where to eat, what to see, and the best way to spend your time the way you want to in the Fredericksburg area. Call (703) 371–5666.

Allman's Bar B Q, at 2000 Augustine Avenue just of Jeff Davis Hwy., is one of those places people like so much they don't want to tell too many people about it. Pete White has been running this hole-in-the-wall with about eight tables and eight stools since the mid-fifties, and it's famous for its barbecue pork. A sandwich goes for $1.75, a huge platter is $5.95, and when all the pork is gone, Allman's closes down for the day. Pete says he tried to stay open after the barbecue was finished, to serve hamburgers and such, but people just weren't interested. You can order other things, such as hamburgers, and the milk shakes are delicious ($1.25 for regular, $1.50 for thick). He opens at 11:00 A.M. every day except Wednesday, when Allman's is closed. The phone number is (703) 373–9881.

Fredericksburg is surrounded by battlefields and cemeteries, including Fredericksburg, Chancellorsville, Wilderness, and Spotsylvania Courthouse, each with programs run by the National Park Service. Descriptive audiotapes for driving tours are usually available at each headquarters building. Get directions from the Fredericksburg Visitor Center.

The National Park Service Visitor Center, the starting place for a self-guided tour through Fredericksburg and Spotsylvania Civil

War battlefields, is open daily from 9:00 A.M. to 5:00 P.M. with extended hours during the summer months. A small museum includes an orientation program and some exhibits. There is no admission charge. Guided tours of the Sunken Road are given three times daily in the summer. The visitors center is located at Lafayette Boulevard and Sunken Road. The Chancellorsville Visitor Center is located off Route 3 west and is open from 9:00 A.M. to 5:00 P.M. daily; Write P.O. Box 679, Fredericksburg 22404 or call (703) 373-4461.

Falmouth, about a mile outside of Fredericksburg, offers a popular Historic Walking Tour in late October that includes private homes and historic spots, an introduction to the village witch, craft demonstrations, and usually music and street dancing.

Gari Melchers, one of America's finest impressionist painters, lived at Belmont from 1916 until his death in 1932. The home now houses the Memorial Gallery, where spacious rooms are filled with antiques and paintings by Melchers and others, such as Jan Breugel, Frans Snyders, Auguste Rodin, and Berthe Morisot.

Belmont is closed Tuesday and Thursday year-round, and Christmas and New Year's. During the summer (April 1 through September 30), it's open from 10:00 A.M. to 5:00 P.M. and Sunday from 1:00 P.M. to 5:00 P.M. Winter hours are 10:00 A.M. to 4:00 P.M. Admission is $1.50 for adults and 50¢ for children 6 through 18. To get there from Interstate 95, take the Falmouth-Warrenton exit onto Highway 17 east, go 1¼ miles to Route 1001 (just before the flashing light), and turn right to Belmont. From the Fredericksburg Visitor Center, drive north on Highway 17 (Caroline Street). After crossing the Rappahannock River, turn left at the traffic light in Falmouth and go ¼ mile up the hill and turn left on Route 1001 to Belmont. For more information call (703) 373-3634.

Off the Beaten Path in Tidewater Virginia

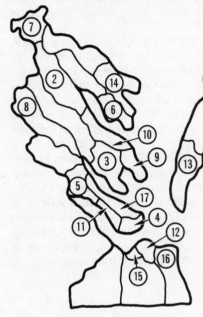

1. Accomack County
     Wallops Island
     National Wildlife Refuge
     Refuge Waterfowl Museum
     Oyster Museum of Chincoteague
     Owl Restaurant and Motel
     Debtors Prison
2. Essex County
     Lowery's Restaurant
     Wall's Wood Shed
3. Gloucester County
     Gloucester's Courthouse
     Virginia Institute of Marine Science
4. Hampton
     Casemate Museum
     Chamberlin Hotel
     Syms-Eaton Museum and
        Kecoughtan Indian Village
     NASA Visitor Center
5. James City County
     Carter's Grove

6. Lancaster County
     Mary Ball Washington Museum
        and Library
     The Tides Inn
7. King George County
     Camillo Vineyards
8. King William County
     Pamunkey Indian Reservation
9. Mathews County
     Donk's
10. Middlesex County
     Urbanna Oyster Festival
11. Newport News
     Mariners Museum
     Virginia Living Museum
12. Norfolk
     Norfolk Botanical Gardens
     Wells Theatre
     Chrysler Museum
13. Northampton County
     Etz Seafood Restaurant
14. Northumberland County
     Sunnybank Ferry
     Smith Island Cruise
15. Portsmouth
     Virginia's Sports Hall of Fame
16. Virginia Beach
     Mt. Trashmore
     Cashvan's Horse Farm
     Old Cape Henry Lighthouse
     Virginia Marine Science Museum
     Virginia Brewing Company
17. York County
     Yorktown Shipwreck Archaelogical
        Project
     Nick's Seafood Pavilion
     Jamestown Festival Park

Tidewater Virginia

America started here with the 1607 settlement of Jamestown. Battles were fought to defend our right to exist. Shipping, vital to our continuance, came through these ports. Our reliance on the Virginia waterfront—for recreation and pleasure—is just as strong today.

You can visit almost all of the nearly 400 years since Jamestown was settled. Start at the Jamestown Festival Park and see the replicas of the three ships that sailed over with what we assume was so little knowledge. (And remember that a modern day crew, with many technological advances, could not duplicate the feat.) Go to Williamsburg to see the colonial capital. Stop by Norfolk to see the results of merchants and chandlers plying their wares. Stop by majestic plantations and Indian villages. Jump light years ahead with a visit to the NASA space centers at Wallops and Hampton where our space exploration began. Then settle back into a comfortable time in the little hamlets and towns that dot the Eastern Shore and the Northern Neck. Whatever it offers, you can be sure its finest offering will be the food brought from the sea and served any way you care to try it. Hook or snag or rake it yourself and cook it yourself; or just enjoy the labors of someone else bringing in the catch and preparing it for you.

Accomack County

This county and Northampton County compose the Virginia portion of the Eastern Shore. The dozens of hamlets in these two counties are known for their surf and deepwater fishing, seafood, crafters, sweet potatoes, chicken, and a grand welcome to those who are "come here's" (families who have been in Virginia for less than three generations).

Almost all directions are given as "off Route 13," for that is the main highway through this area. There are several "searoads," which basically parallel the highway, such as Route 316 on the bay (Chesapeake) side and Routes 600 and 604 on the sea (Atlantic Ocean) side. It's along these roads that you'll find some of the unique Eastern Shore architecture, including those with four different roof levels referred to as "big house, little house, colonnade, and kitchen."

Many people come for the most popular draw, or at least the best known, the pony roundup and penning at Chincoteague. Others want sun and sand or the antiques and the duck decoys. They're all available here. Our advice on the decoys is to look at quite a few first so you can decide what you want. There are decorative decoys (they look pretty) and working decoys (those that were hollowed out and had weights placed on the bottom for balance in the water and were used to lure ducks to the blinds, which can also be quite beautiful). Some are brand-new and machine turned (you can even assemble and paint them yourself), some have intricately carved feather structures, and some are old and drab looking. You can expect to pay from $50 to $700 or more.

To get to Wallops Island, Chincoteague, and Assateague Island, turn east off of Route 13 at T's Corner, where there's a Mears drug and general store, onto Route 175.

Wallops Island is occupied by the National Aeronautics and Space Administration's Goddard Space Flight Center. This was the nation's first rocket firing and testing station, and it's possible the flight center could be used for commercial satellite launches within the next five years. The site is geared toward small launchings, making it less expensive and easier for private firms to use than the Kennedy Space Center in Florida. Patented to John Wallop in 1672, Wallops Island became a National Advisory Committee for Aeronautics (NACA) site for aerodynamic research, while part of it was leased to the Navy for aviation ordnance testing. The NACA eventually became NASA, which took over the site when the Chincoteague Naval Air Station nearby closed at the end of World War II.

You're invited inside the NASA museum for a self-guided tour that can last from fifteen minutes to several hours. (Groups of more than twenty are asked to make advance reservations.) There's an Apollo XVII moon rock sample collected by astronaut Jack Schmitt from near the landing site in the Taurus-Littrow Valley region of the moon. Films, one on the forty-year history of Wallops Island and one on space highlights, are shown on a regular basis. Unlike some other space and government areas, cameras are encouraged at this facility. The gift shop sells postcards, plates, cups, mugs, books, T- shirts, patches, and other spaceflight souvenirs. There are 100 to 150 space launches a year set from Wallops, but there's little or no advance schedule, you have to stay several miles away, and some of them go up so fast they're off the ground and out of sight before you've blinked your eyes. Model rocket launches are held the first Saturday of every month.

The museum is open Thursday through Monday (closed Tuesday and Wednesday) 10:00 A.M. to 4:00 P.M. and closed Thanksgiving, Christmas, and New Year's. Call (804) 824–5833 or (804) 824–3411, ext. 584 or 298, for advance reservations.

After your NASA visit, you're ready to drive the last few miles to Chincoteague ("beautiful land across the water") and the nearby Assateague Island. Once in Chincoteague you'll find lots of places to shop and eat and a variety of other activities (if your visit is scheduled around Easter weekend, you can attend the Annual Chincoteague Decoy Festival), but the main focus is on the **National Wildlife Refuge.**

Is there a soul alive who has not read the book, seen the movie, or in some way heard about Misty, Marguerite Henry's famed horse from Chincoteague? Only a handful more haven't heard about the annual (since 1925) Firefighters' Pony Penning and swim held to sell off some of the horses to keep the herd at a manageable size. Thousands attend this event at the carnival grounds, which is held the last Wednesday and Thursday of July. The wild ponies, which are assumed to be descended from mustangs that swam ashore from a wrecked Spanish ship in the sixteenth century, are auctioned by members of the volunteer fire department on Chincoteague. The members dress up in cowboy garb and corral the ponies, then carefully supervise them as the horses swim to Chincoteague where they sell for about $200 each. For more information contact the Chamber of Commerce, Box 258, Chincoteague Island 23336, (804) 336–6161. How nice to be able to visit Misty's relatives and stroll alongside them as they munch the grass of this seashore wildlife refuge that is their home.

Throughout the refuge you can take hikes, ride bikes, sit in the sun, and enjoy yourself. There's a 3.5-mile bicycle-hiking loop open dawn to dusk for pedestrians and bikes (no mopeds allowed) and on which autos are allowed from 3:00 P.M. to dusk. Some 250 different birds fly by, and snow geese can be seen most of fall and winter. In September the refuge is a major resting and feeding area for the endangered peregrine falcon. Forest underbrush has been cleared in some areas, and nesting boxes constructed for the endangered Delmarva fox squirrel. The sika, an oriental elk, Virginia whitetail deer, and, of course, small bands of wild ponies are scattered throughout the refuge.

Going back toward Route 13, you can see a huge selection of working duck decoys at the **Refuge Waterfowl Museum.** You'll see weapons, boats, traps, art, and items related to the life of the watermen, but what you'll really see are some magnificent duck decoy carvings. You might find the work of artisans Paul E. Fisher (Suffolk), Penny Miller (Reston), Reggie Birch (Chincoteague), J. D. Sprankle (Annapolis, Maryland), Paul Nock (Salisbury, Maryland), Tim Gorman (Machipongo), David and Ann-Marie Bundick (Modest Town), Walter W. Oler, Sr. (Chincoteague), and noted master carver Grayson Chesser. Delbert "Cigar" Daisey is the resident carver. He earned his nickname when Game Warden John Bucklew found a handful of cigar wrappers in a robbed trap Bucklew had set for banding and was able to trace them back to Daisey.

Among the exhibits are backbay and canvas-covered Canada geese decoys, sink box decoys made of cast iron and used as weights on a sink box to make it float with a low profile, and a table with signatures from the Swan Club. You'll also see a model of a reed and feathers decoy made by Indians almost 1,000 years ago, handcrafted by Dr. H. S. Doolittle.

John Maddox owns the museum, which opened in 1977. Wyle Maddox, builder of the bridge to Assateague and for whom Maddox Boulevard is named, rode with the fire department in the Annual July Roundup and appeared in the movie *Misty* in his real-life role as leader of the cowboys. Wyle loved to duck hunt and was instrumental in the museum's acquiring this site for its building and collection.

The museum is open daily 10:00 A.M. to 5:00 P.M. Admission is $1.50 for adults and $.50 for children under 13. It's located a block east of the only traffic circle on the island on Maddox Boulevard, just before the bridge before entering the Wildlife Refuge. Call (804) 336–5800.

Open only in the summer is the **Oyster Museum of Chincoteague,** said to be the only one of its kind in the United States. Since 1972 it has featured live marine exhibits of clams, oysters, crabs, starfish, sea horses, and other marine specimens, as well as historical and maritime artifacts, shell specimens, implements of the seafood industry and of the shucking process, and an area diorama with lights and sound. The Oyster Museum covers a history of the Chincoteague and Assateague area and preserves the culture of the islands and of Eastern Shore oystering (the prime industry of the island) from the 1600s to the present. It holds the Maddox Library papers for marine life.

The museum, located along the Assateague Beach Road, is open daily from 11:00 A.M. to 5:00 P.M. during the summer months and weekends only during early spring and fall. Admission is $1 for adults and $.50 for children. The phone number is (804) 336-6117.

Carrying a mailing address of Parksley, the **Owl Restaurant and Motel** is located on Route 13, about 2 miles east of Parksley. It's been owned by the Roache family since 1937 and now is managed by John and Tony Roache. You're sure to find the definitive crab cake here, prepared according to their mother Josephine's recipe. We're not sure what holds the cake together, for it's difficult (if not impossible) to find any filler. Meals, some with homemade spoonbread, are huge and reasonably priced, but don't order too much, for you'll want some of her chocolate rum pie in a meringue crust. You can buy a whole pie for $14 ($3 for the glass pie plate, which is refunded when you return the plate). The local residents gather here for breakfast and three to four dinner meals a week. The tables next to the booth under the "shooting the bull" sign, made by Tony, generally are taken by these local farmers, but there's nothing that says you can't sit there. For hours, call (804) 665-5191.

Parksley's newest railroad depot was acquired in 1988 from Nancy Shield of Accomac. She agreed to give the depot from Hopeton, a small village about 2 miles north of Parksley, if the town would use it for a museum. The last time a depot was here was in the late sixties and it was a little larger than this 60-foot version, but the town is grateful because it is in such good condition. Dozens of citizens have donated their time to clean the site, paint and electrify the station, as well as having donated a potbellied stove, a railroad safe, a spike hammer, railroad lanterns, a railroad jack, a depot ceiling fan, and more than $20,000 toward the museum. A 1943 caboose was donated by the Norfolk Southern Corporation, and the Tidewater chapter of the National Historical Railway Society promised a railway baggage car. All of this will celebrate the history of the train on the Eastern Shore, when that was *the* form of transportation and the only way to ship things in and out of the area.

The second largest restored town next to Williamsburg is Accomac. The Chamber of Commerce office (c. 1816) is a historic landmark. Talk with Margaret Porterfield, executive director of the Eastern Shore Tourism Commission, at No. 1 Courthouse Avenue (804–787–2460), about your specific interests.

Another historic landmark in Accomac, on Route 764, is the **Debtors Prison,** c. 1783, a two-story and loft building with a high pitched roof and Flemish Bond pattern to the brickwork. The west chimney is an inside unit to conserve heat. Even if the building isn't open, you can peek into the windows to see the two rooms on the first floor. One room has been furnished as it might have been when John Snead, the resident jailer, and his family lived there between 1806 and 1815. The other will recall days when the building was a prison for debtors. When the General Assembly prohibited jailing for debts, the building was used for a variety of purposes including storage, a public library (1911–1927), scout headquarters, and WPA workroom, until 1953 when the Drummondtown Branch of the Association for the Preservation of Virginia Antiquities received custody of the building and repaired and restored it to be a museum. Call (703) 787–2460 for details.

Dr. William H. Turner, born and raised on the Eastern Shore and now the local dentist and artisan-owner of the Chesapeake Bay Wildlife Designs in Onley, creates outstanding wildlife bronzes (otters with turtle, canvasbacks, Canada goose, whitetail deer, mallards), most in very limited editions. He creates the design and then the mold from which his magnificent animals are produced, using the lost wax system. Almost all of his work is on consignment or commission, and if you see three bronze fish in the new Virginia Science Museum in Virginia Beach you'll know Dr. Turner made them. Ditto for a huge wildcat in the Naples, Florida, museum. Much of his work is sold through one-man charity shows across the country.

Also on display at the shop are the small animals of Virginia's forested Eastern Shore, sculpted by artist David Turner. Each finely detailed piece is created in high quality pewter and hand finished to a lustrous patina. Included in his collection are the gray squirrel, red fox, river otter, opossum with young, racoon, and cottontail.

Most of the sales are by mail order, but you're invited to stop by to browse or shop daily from 8:00 A.M. to 5:00 P.M. If you'd like a tour of the facility (which used to be a steak house) and a chance to see workers at their crafts, stop by during office hours. Write for a catalog to Chesapeake Bay Wildlife Designs, Ltd., P.O. Box 128, Onley, VA 23418. The shop is on southbound Route 13; (804) 787–4431.

The Locustville Academy Museum, on Route 605 in the Academy Building, is the only remaining school of higher learning of about a dozen that existed on the Eastern Shore during the 1800s, and the weatherboarding, brick foundations, and interior are intact. The school provided advance studies for college-bound students or those entering business at a far lower cost than boarding schools. Advanced courses included Latin, Greek, and French, and in 1862 tuition did not exceed $20 for a semester. The school operated from the fall of 1859 until 1879 (except for brief periods during the Civil War) and apparently looks much as it did when it was in operation, although the original entrance road has been closed. Inside are an old teacher's desk and students' desks, old textbooks, photographs, documents, and historical artifacts from the area.

Wachapreague, off Route 605 just south of Route 180, bills itself as the "Flounder Capital of the World," and this fishing resort is said to have the state's largest charter boat marina, with all the wonderful fishing tournaments that accompany so many people involved in such a delightful sport. Call (804) 787–4110 for details.

For fresh shellfish and shellfish products, you have to stop by George Spence's place near Quinby. During the summer, you'll find him in the large complex of low-lying buildings just before you cross the wooden-slated, tar-covered bridge over the Machipongo River on Route 182. Depending on the season, there will be enormous numbers of soft crab flats stacked about. He'll have hard and soft crabs, crab cakes, bay scallops, sea scallops, squid, minnows, and clams. George has been working this operation since the 1930s, when he was in his teens. His wife, Marie, picks crabs during the week and makes about 300–400 crab cakes on Saturday. If he's closed, stop by his house. Just continue down Route 182 until just before it ends. His house is on the left, the one with the paved driveway. The number is (804) 442–9553.

Essex County

The small town of Tappahannock on the Rappahannock River was founded in 1680, the same year as Philadelphia, and has seen several name changes before settling on this Indian name meaning rise and fall of water. Thirteen buildings are on the Historic Register, and you can walk the streets (which still carry their original names) to view the buildings, which include the Old Debtor's Prison on Prince Street between Church and Cross streets, which now serves as the county treasurer's office. Most are not usually open for inspection. The Confederate Soldier statue on Prince Street in Tappahannock, a common memorial in many Virginia cities, lists all the local men who fought in the war. A booklet entitled *Essex County Virginia—Its Historic Homes, Landmarks and Traditions* is for sale at the library, or you can talk with Catherine Pendleton DeShazo of the Tappahannock–Essex County Chamber of Commerce (804-443-2717) about the buildings and other attractions in the area.

For some time, when you approached Tappahannock on Route 17, you could note a sign with the legend "You are approaching Tappannock—home of 1,200 happy souls and one old sorehead." The sign apparently fell victim to highway beautification regulations, and the sorehead fell victim to time and age.

Reportedly, the old sorehead was father to William and Rob Lowery, and a visit to Tappahannock isn't a visit without a stop at their place, **Lowery's Restaurant** on Church Street. Here you'll meet William Lowery and his younger brother, Robert. People are working there who worked there in the early 1940s (the restaurant opened in 1938), and they're now "feeding our third generation." Rockfish was the number one item (perhaps after the famed Rappahannock oysters) on the menu until catching and serving them from the Chesapeake Bay waters and tributaries was banned to help increase their population. But the rockfish shall return. In the meantime, try one of the seafood platters. The food is pretty good, and the servings are much too generous to eat at one sitting.

Within the building, part of which used to be the site of a garage where Kaisers, Fraziers, and Packards were sold, you'll find a gift shop, antique cars, and a bird that meows (a cat stayed by its door all night), and, of course, the restaurant. The cars used to be their father's hobby. The old garage was torn down in 1980 when more dining space was needed. After Mr. Lowery's death, the "boys" decided to keep the cars and put them in the restaurant so they wouldn't have to be "taken out every day" so people could see them. Two of the cars are still in running condition. There's also a Model-A with about 15,000 miles that isn't on display. Also on exhibit is a collection of Tappahannock postcards that includes a picture of the first Rappahannock bridge built in 1927. You can buy their own salad dressings. Their phone number is (804) 443–2920.

Heading south on Route 360 toward Richmond, you'll pass **Wall's Wood Shed** on the northbound side. Inside you'll find JoAnne and Bill Wall, makers of wooden toys and children's furniture. They didn't always make toys; they used to do some furniture refinishing and custom woodworking. In the late 1970s, says JoAnne, "somebody asked us to make a truck; somebody else wanted something else and one thing led to another," and in August 1978 they were completely in toys. They make doll cradles, teddy bears (real popular), airplanes, rocking horses, old-fashioned pull toys, floating boats, and little tote chairs, all from their own patterns. They take their toys to shows from Leesburg to Virginia Beach (and as far as Tennessee) and there are times, they say, just before a big show or the holidays, when it feels as though they're at the toy-making business twenty-four and twenty-six hours a day.

JoAnne does most of the finish work and some of the lighter woodwork, such as puzzles and little cars. Bill does most of the heavy woodworking. They use kiln-dried heavy yellow Virginia and North Carolina pine and West Coast sugar pine. They don't wholesale; their sales are through shows and special orders. When they do sell to a store, it's at full price. The cradle or high chair sells for $29.50, the rocking horse, $49.50. Prices start at $1.50; napkin rings are $2.50. "Very few people copy us because we paint ours, we finish our toys, and nobody's going to sit up until 4:00 A.M. painting an airplane the way we do," says JoAnne.

Do stop by and browse or shop. They're open every day, except weekends when they're at shows. The number is (804) 443–4455.

Gloucester County

Gloucester County is the home of the annual Daffodil Show, sometime between early March and mid-April (depending on the growing season) when the fields are abloom with these gorgeous messengers of spring; (804) 693–2425. Gloucester County is also the home of two of America's oldest churches, Ware Church (c. 1690, with an interesting graveyard and beautiful paintings, open for Sunday services) and Abingdon Church (c. 1755, with beautiful brickwork, open grounds, and services on Sunday), and of some marvelous homes that are privately owned but open to the public during Garden Week. (This is one of a series of events scheduled throughout the state during the fourth week of April. Call the Garden Club of Virginia (804–644–7776) for additonal information.)

Gloucester is the birthplace of Dr. Walter Reed, and his home is one of the buildings maintained by the Association for the Preservation of Virginia Antiquities. The grounds are open to visitors daily, and the building is open on social occasions or by appointment (804–642–2587).

You can see more of Walter Reed in **Gloucester's Courthouse** (c. 1766), which is part of the historic county seat complex. As you enter the courthouse, turn right and go to the back of the building. There you'll find two large format scrapbooks with photographs of historic people from Gloucester, including Dr. Reed, Maj. J. N. Stuggs, Miss Cornelia Thornton (she died overseas in World War I, the first American nurse to be buried in English soil and the first nurse from Virginia to be given special military honors at Arlington National Cemetery), Sheriff James Dabney, Commonwealth Attorney Maryus Jones, Speaker Augustine Warner, House of Burgesses, Lt. Colonel Fielding, Lewis Taylor, C.S.A., and many others.

All five buildings in the complex have been in continuous use and are now used by county officials; it is open weekdays 8:30 A.M. to 4:30 P.M. Stop by The Village Secretary and the Chamber of Commerce, run by Judith E. Brabrand, for more detailed information.

Drive off Route 17, following the signs for the **Virginia Institute of Marine Science** (VIMS), but for just a moment keep on driving down to the water. Gloucester Point is a great place for a photographic or otherwise appreciative view of the Yorktown River Bridge. Now drive back to the new VIMS museum building, part of the College of William and Mary, to see their interactive displays and exhibits (where you can pick up or touch some of the hardier species, such as crabs), freshwater to higher-salinity aquariums (complete with shark and maybe even the beautiful single spot butterfly fish), and demonstrations about sea life, all under the direction of Joe M. Choromanski, aquarium curator. Pete Foley, a local taxidermist, has made and will be making some fiberglass reproductions of some of the animals they are not going to be able to display.

VIMS is open daily from 10:00 A.M. to 4:00 P.M., with a possibility of an extension to 6:00 P.M. during the summer. Be sure to ask for a complete set of some great seafood recipe brochures, at no charge. Write to VIMS, Gloucester Point 23062 or call (804) 642-7174.

Country flea markets hold such an appeal to city folk, so it's no wonder that Stagecoach Flea Market and Antiques has been drawing eager buyers and curious day-trippers from several states for ten years. About forty-five shops are open on weekends on the nearly twelve-acre site. Treasures and junk can be found here for prices near and dear or at a steal. New merchandise arrives every week, but some of it has been sitting around for quite a while. Be careful of your impulse buying if you see a "hold" sign on something that you suddenly must have. Although it is not unheard of elsewhere, some of the dealers have been known to try to tempt your wallet with this ploy, when no one really has requested the hold except the dealer. Stagecoach owner Harris Holland says bargaining is acceptable. Stagecoach is in Gloucester, about 9½ miles north of the Coleman Bridge on Route 17. It is open from 9:00 A.M. to 5:00 P.M. Saturday and Sunday, all year.

Hampton County

The Hampton Visitors Center has moved into its new facilities, and staff are here to answer your questions about area attractions and accommodations. Brochures and maps are available. Cruises of the Hampton Roads Harbor, Fort Wool, and the Norfolk Naval Station also are available. Open daily, from 9:00 A.M. to 5:00 P.M., except major holidays; (804) 727-6108.

The **Casemate Museum,** set in an impressive location—a cavern of rooms built within the thick walls of Fort Monroe—relates the battles of Hampton Roads, particularly during the Civil War. The story of the *Monitor* and *Merrimac* battle is told here. You can walk through the fort, the third oldest in America, and take a look at the Old Point Comfort Lighthouse, built in 1802 and in continous use since then. Fort Algernoume was on this site from 1609 to 1667. Fort George was built in 1727 and destroyed by a hurricane in 1749. Weakened coastal defenses during the War of 1812 allowed the British to sack Hampton and capture Washington by sailing up the Chesapeake Bay. Fort Monroe, completely surrounded by a moat and the largest stone fort ever constructed on this continent,

Old Point Comfort Lighthouse

was started in 1819. Quarters Number One, stop nine on the tour of the fort, was built shortly after 1819 and is the oldest building at the fort. It's been in use since 1823. Write to P.O. Box 341, Fort Monroe 23651. Follow the signs off Interstate 64. The phone number is (804) 727–3971.

The Zero Mile Post at Fort Monroe is a replica of the original post that stood at Fort Monroe on Old Point Comfort, marking the end of the track on the Chesapeake and Ohio Railway, from which point all main line distances have been measured.

The **Chamberlin Hotel** is one of the venerable places, a "Grand Old Lady of the Chesapeake" of the hotel world. Located next to Fort Monroe at Old Point Comfort, it started life as the Hygeia Hotel (named after the Greek goddess of health) in 1820. Under orders from the secretary of war, it was leveled in 1862 after serving as a hospital during the first part of the Civil War. A second Hygeia was started within a year, and the first Chamberlin was built alongside it in 1902. The Chamberlin burned down in March 1920. Marcellus Wright, a renowned Virginia architect, designed the new Georgian-style Chamberlin-Vanderbilt, which opened its doors in 1928 as Virginia's second "fireproof" hotel (the first was the Stonewall Jackson in Staunton). Owners Vernon and Mary Stuart have spent millions of dollars in renovating, restoring, and redecorating.

Food service is a special treat in the Great Gatsby (live dance music) and draws many guests who are not staying at the hotel, so reservations are suggested. There are two saltwater pools (one indoors, one outdoors), two tennis courts, bicycles for a picturesque cycle tour of the historic Fort Monroe, a sauna and Jacuzzi, a game room, and fishing. Al Murphy and Phil Merrick (retired colonels with thirty-two and twenty-six years of military service respectively) manage the facility.

The Chamberlin even has a museum! Apparently people have had dance cards (you remember when gentlemen requested a specific dance from a lady and that request was entered on a dance card), photographs (there's an exceptional series of the fire) and other memorabilia in attics all over the place. Now they realize their kids don't want the stuff, so they've been giving it back to the Chamberlin. Although the hotel has received boxes and boxes of materials, they're still looking, so if you have an item or some items you wish to contribute, let them know. There's no admission charge for the museum, which is located behind the Chamberlin's gift shop and therefore is accessible only when the gift shop is open. The hours vary and are posted on the gift shop door. For information, call (804) 723–6511 or toll-free, (800) 446–1045 (outside Virginia) or (800) 582–8975 (inside Virginia).

Hampton's history starts with the Indians and continues through pirates, colonization, the Revolutionary War, and the War Between the States. The **Syms-Eaton Museum and Kecoughtan Indian Village** has a number of audiovisual presentations that relate the history of Hampton. Additionally, there is a recreation of an Eastern Woodland Indian Village, and tours are provided on the hour, weather permitting. Visitors learn about the lifestyles, culture, and history of the Kecoughtan Indians, who inhabited Hampton 400 years ago.

Open from 10:00 A.M. to 3:00 P.M., Monday through Friday and noon to 4:00 P.M. on Saturday and Sunday, they recommend you allow one hour for the Syms-Eaton Museum and thirty minutes for the Kecoughtan Indian Village. No admission charge. The location is 418 West Mercury Boulevard in Hampton. Call (804) 727–6248 for details.

The Phoebus Post Office **WPA mural** by William Calfee (who also did one of the Petersburg murals, and those in Tazewell and Harrisonburg) was done in 1941 and is entitled *Chesapeake Fishermen,* a rather self-explanatory title.

The **NASA Visitor Center,** at Langley Research Center, features interesting displays about aviation history, safety, wind tunnels, and aerodynamics and about how theory can test the structural integrity of a new or revised design so people and companies don't risk lots of money and lives. Langley started in 1917 as the Langley Memorial Aeronautical Laboratory, and the first seven astronauts received their training here.

In the museum there are some hands-on displays, some hanging displays, the *Apollo 12* command module, a space suit, a $1/15$ scale model of the space shuttle *Columbia,* a moon rock, and a few computer quizzes to test your knowledge of aviation history. Films are shown periodically, but the absolutely most fascinating part of the museum is the television hookup used during the preparation and deployment of a space shuttle launch. Seeing it is like being on the launching pad or even in the shuttle itself. There is a gift shop and a picnic area. "Flight Deck of the Future" is a new exhibit at the NASA Langley Visitor Center. Watch as a typical airline cockpit turns into a cockpit of the future with the push of a button. This new complex computer flight system now being tested by NASA will be used by commercial airlines within the next fifteen years.

The NASA Visitor Center is open Monday through Saturday from 8:30 A.M. to 4:30 P.M. and Sunday from noon to 4:30 P.M. and closed New Year's Day, Easter, Thanksgiving, and Christmas. For more information, write NASA Visitor Center, Langley Research Center, Mail Stop 480, Hampton 23665–5225 or call (804) 865–2855. There's no admission charge.

James City County

In 1984 a new 92,000-square-foot reception center was opened for **Carter's Grove** (near Hampton), once a 300,000-acre plantation where Robert "King" Carter's grandson built a mansion in the 1750s. The new facility has a ticket and information desk, a 100-seat theater, an exhibit gallery, a gift shop, a vending area and rest rooms. After a brief orientation film, shown about every twenty minutes (last showing is at 4:20 P.M.), you cross a deep wooded ravine via a footbridge to the mansion or to an overlook for an introductory presentation of the archaeological dig of the site of Wolstenholme Towne, an early seventeenth-century settlement. From there you can hear descriptions at nine barrel-housed stations around the grounds about the items that have been found and how they are used to document the partial reconstruction of palisades, fences, and buildings. Most of these sites were explored between 1976 and 1981, but diggers are still waiting for one site to reveal its historical significance.

That mess of ships in the James River, across from Ft. Eustis, is not part of the Navy's "mothball" fleet but belongs to the United States Department of Transportation Maritime Administration. The ships are sealed for dehumidification, safety, and security. They have been coated with a thick oil base paint that rusts and peels but *protects* the ships. Unfortunately, this is not a shopping center of used boats, although occasionally one of them will be sold for use as an artificial reef. In emergency, one assumes, they could be mobilized for national defense.

King George County

Camillo Vineyards is one of several vineyards where you can either pick your own grapes for wine making or buy them already picked. You cannot, however, buy wine here, only the makings for it. Beverly and Tom Iezzi operate this farm, which produces Chardonnay, Niagara, Villard Blanc, Chenin Blanc white grapes, and Chelois, Concord, Chambourcin, and Cabernet Sauvignon red grapes. You must call ahead for the fall picking during August and September, and you should bring your own containers. A crusher and press are available for use at the vineyard. Fresh grape juice, ready to drink or ferment, is available in gallon or five-gallon increments. A complete inventory of winemaking supplies is available.

To get there from Fredericksburg, take Route 3 east to Route 206 (approximately 16 miles) and turn left to Owens (8 miles). Turn left on Route 624, which takes a sharp left to Owens (8 miles). Turn left on Route 624, which takes a sharp left turn after 2 miles, for a total of 4 miles. Turn left at Route 687. Go 1 1/2 miles to the Iezzi mailbox, with a barrel and an Italian flag, on the right. Follow the dirt and then gravel road to the end. For more information call (703) 663-2577.

King William County

The **Pamunkey Indian Museum** is under the leadership of Chief T. D. Cook. Inside the museum you'll find several nice displays (and a videotape) about the Pamunkey people and their way of life, from the Ice Age to the present. These people were members of the tribe under the leadership of Chief Powhatan (the name he told the settlers), who was the father of Pocahontas. Some of the items in the fifteen display windows are original, some are as it's assumed they were. There are some interesting items for sale by Katie Southward (Laughing Breeze), Daisy Bradby (Redwing), Dora Bradby (Laughing Water), and Bernice Langston (Evening Breeze) in the gift shop, including a new pottery form for the Pamunkey, which is glazed and burned, as well as the older coil method, and if you time your visit right, you might see a demonstration.

The museum is open 9:00 A.M. to 4:00 P.M. Monday through Saturday and 1:00 P.M. to 5:00 P.M. on Sunday, but not on major holidays. The museum may not open exactly on time, but stay around a few minutes and someone will come by. Admission is $1 for adults and 50¢ for children 6-13, seniors, and school groups. Picnic tables are available. It's located about 10 miles off Route 30 (off Interstate 95) on Route 633 and then Route 673, past the Lanesville cemetery and over the railroad tracks. The road turns, but the signs are easy to follow. The phone number is (804) 843–4792 or (804) 843–2851.

Lancaster County

The **Mary Ball Washington Museum and Library** in Lancaster has a marvelous display of fashions from 1818 until 1929, including a wedding dress from 1888 by Thalhimers in a lovely display organized by curator Susan Hudgins, an excellent genealogical library, a historical lending library, programs, workshops, and films. Organized to honor the Lancaster County–born mother of George Washington, it's located in the Lancaster House (c. 1798), which was lovingly restored by the Lancaster Woman's Club. Next to it is the Old Jail (c. 1819) and the Old Clerk's Office (1797). The museum, on Route 3, is open Monday through Friday, 10:00 A.M. to 4:00 P.M. There is no admission charge, but donations (of money or appropriate historical memorabilia) are accepted. Call for more information: (804) 462–7280.

Merry Point Ferry, one of four remaining river ferries in Virginia (in operation since 1668), rides across the western branch of the Corotoman River. For years the *Arminta* had plied these waters, carrying three small cars or two regular size cars and taking about ten or fifteen minutes to cross, but the *Lancaster,* a new, all-in-one steel boat and scow has been installed. The *Arminta* carried 12,229 vehicles in 1984 at a cost of $53,943. Taking the ferry from Corotoman to Ottoman will land you in the town of Lively.

The ferry runs from 7:00 A.M. to 7:00 P.M. (if daylight) daily except Sunday (it may not operate at times of extreme tides or adverse weather). There's no charge to the passengers. Take Route 604 off of either Route 3 or Route 354.

On August 17, 1985, the new post office at Merry Point on Route 604 (formerly Slater's Corner) opened under the direction of Betty Beane, postmaster since 1976. It's open from 8:00 A.M. until noon, Monday through Saturday, and you can get a souvenir postcard with an artistic rendition of the previous post office, which is ferry-side of the present location (it was at the ferry dock in 1846).

Irvington is the home of **The Tides Inn,** billed as one of America's most outstanding small resorts, a claim we won't argue. We could fill a book with personal service stories we've experienced and experienced by our friends and people we've sent to the inn. Combining a competent staff and resort facilities, the Tides Inn is a blend of remoteness and convenience—only 8 miles up the Rappahannock by private yacht and only about an hour's drive from Williamsburg, Richmond, and Norfolk—a contradiction that begs to be forgiven. People who come to this part of the country are coming to the Tides Inn, which is well worth getting out of the main channel or off the Interstate to visit. There are forty-five holes of golf, tennis, boating of all types, swimming, dancing, fine dining, and, best of all, an informal elegance.

The inn is closed from early January through about Easter weekend. Owner Bob Lee Stephens issues a sporadic newsletter to keep you informed of all the activities, special events, and plans for the upcoming year. At this point, he's thinking about installing television in the guest rooms, an absolutely abhorrent idea to him. He says, "I think I have come up with a way that we can hide the darn things, yet if you really want to see TV in the privacy of your room, you can." Call (804) 438–5000; (800) TIDES INN (east of the Mississippi); or (800) 552–3461 (in Virginia).

Mathews County

Paul Hudgins worked for the government for many years before he decided he wanted to do something that would allow him to be his own boss. He went back to school and now makes Paul's Point Honey, which he sells on the steps of the Mathews County Courthouse in Mathews on Thursday, Friday, and Saturday. A pint of his wildflower honey is $2.45, a quart is $4.65, and a half gallon is $8.90. He also sells beeswax. You can stop by his place by driving east on Route 14 (past the right-hand turn when it meets with Route 198) and turning south on Route 621 until it narrows and you've almost run out of paved road. His home is the one on the right with the long dirt driveway (804–725–5185). **Donk's** is the place where everyone (504 seats and 70 chairs in the aisles) goes on alternate Saturday nights—"Virginia's Little Ole Opry." This is the place that three generations of Smiths have operated and that

Betsy Smith Ripley describes as where "big name stars and home-town favorites combine to make terrific shows." With her sister, Joanna Mullis, their aunt, Harriet Smith Farmer, and Uncle Jimmy Smith, they've kept things busy. Some of the stars who have appeared there are Kitty Wells, the Kendalls, the Whites, Becky Hobbs, and Larry Boone. On alternate Saturdays you'll find this family group and their merry troupe, The Shades of Country, at the state fair, a seafood festival, or some other celebration where country music is on the schedule. Obviously, you'll have to call to find out whether this Saturday is the "alternate" one (804–725–7760 or 804–725–3384). The doors open at 7:30 P.M., and the show starts at 8:00 P.M. On Route 198 west of the Route 14 intersection.

Middlesex County

Urbanna, one of America's original harbor towns (established in 1673), enjoys a population of about 600 and a marvelously pictur-esque setting. It's known as the home of the **Urbanna Oyster Festival,** for thousands (perhaps 25,000) come to the little harbor on Urbanna Creek every first weekend in November to harvest the famous oyster beds on the Rappahannock River. From here, oys-ters are sold by the bushel, processed, packed, frozen, and shipped all over. During the festival there are a dozen or so street stands where you can find oysters fried, stewed, on the half shell, roasted, ready to shuck yourself, or in chowder.

Down the road is Deltaville, "the Boatbuilding Capital of the Chesapeake." At one time there were more than twenty boat builders in this area, many of them second and third generation, creating craft that still are used today. Some of the finest houses along the Northern Neck can be found in this area, and a mari-time museum is in the developmental stages.

Newport News

Mary B. Fowler was commissioned to do the five **WPA sculp-tures** in the Newport News Post Office, Courthouse and Customs House on 25th Street at West. They were completed in 1943. The sculptures collectively are called *Captain Newport Bringing News and Aid to the Starting Colonists* and portray progress in agricul-ture, medicine, and other areas of early life in the colonies.

When they say you can discover some of the best craftsmanship on earth at the **Mariners Museum,** believe them. Founded in 1930 by Archer M. Huntington, it contains one of the world's finest collections of figureheads and perhaps the largest figurehead of all time: the Lancaster Eagle, a 3,000- pound gilded eagle (18 1/2-foot wingspan), which was carved by John Haley Bellamy and was on the U.S. frigate *Lancaster* from 1881 to 1921.

August F. Crabtree's collection of sixteen miniature ships (about a quarter inch to the foot) follows the evolution of the sailing ship. Born in 1905 in Oregon, Crabtree was the grandson of a Glasgow shipbuilder. It took Crabtree and his wife, Winnifred (they met when he was building model ships for Hollywood movies and she was painting them), more than twenty-seven years to complete this world-famous collection. The ships are enclosed in glass cases with mirrors underneath so you can see completely around them. Some boards are not in place so you can see inside, and there's a magnifying glass on some so you can appreciate the exacting detail work. This display is worth the visit, all by itself.

But there's more! John Townley, from Northern Neck, comes in a couple of times a week and strolls the museum singing sea chanteys. Guided tours are available, during which time you might hear how Admiral Lord Nelson was shipped home in a wine casket or learn some other interesting military information.

There are twelve galleries featuring decorative arts, ship models, small crafts from workboats to pleasure craft with 100 fascinating full-size boats from around the world, ships' carvings and seapower, as well as a gallery for changing exhibits.

In preparation for its sixtieth anniversary, the museum has begun a program of gallery renovation of the installation of a much-needed new roofing system. To protect artifacts on display, most of the galleries must be closed to the public and dismantled and will remain closed for an extended period. The Decorative Arts, Paintings, Chesapeake Bay, Seapower Gallery, and Changing Exhibits galleries are closed, as is the exhibition "The Immortal Memory: Admiral Horatio Nelson." The Small Craft building is also closed, but for a shorter time period. Simultaneously, construction will continue on a new lobby and Chesapeake Bay exhibition wing and a museum shop. During this interim period, admission rates are lowered to $2.00 for adults, $1.00 for children, $1.50 for senior citizens, military, and AAA adult, and $.75 for military and AAA children. Visitors can still enjoy the fine collection of tall sailing ship figureheads, an exhibit on the Titanic, classic steam engines, an extensive collection of handcrafted models of great passenger steamers and commercial cargo vessels, and the small-craft collection.

There's a 550-acre park, a 165-acre lake, and a gift shop that is open daily. Museum hours are Monday through Saturday, 9:00 A.M. to 5:00 P.M. and Sunday, noon to 5:00 P.M. and closed Christmas. Free conducted tours are offered at 11:00 A.M. Monday through Saturday, and other arrangements can be made. The Mariners Museum is on Museum Drive (off Mercury Boulevard). Call (804) 595–0368.

The newest attraction in Virginia's Hampton Roads area is the **Virginia Living Museum.** It combines the best and most enjoyable elements of a zoological park, science museum, botanical garden, aquarium, and planetarium. They are all in one inspiring, beautiful setting. Hundreds of native American eastern coastal living creatures including mammals, birds, marine life, reptiles, and insects go about their daily routines as you discover the secrets of life in the wild. Indoors, you will find a 60-foot living panorama of the James River, beginning with life in a mountain stream and ending in the amazing depths of the Atlantic. Outdoors, you can stroll amidst the natural beauty of the lakeside forest as a picturesque boardwalk leads you on an up-close safari into the lives of native water animals. You are asked to stay on the paths and to not touch the electric fences.

The museum is open from 9:00 A.M. to 6:00 P.M. Monday through Saturday and 10:00 A.M. to 6:00 P.M. on Sunday from mid-June to Labor Day. Winter hours are the same on weekdays but are 1:00 P.M. to 5:00 P.M. on Sunday. It is open every Thursday evening from 7:00 P.M. to 9:00 P.M. and closed Thanksgiving, Christmas Eve, Christmas Day, and New Year's Day. Combination tickets (for museum/observatory and planetarium) are $5.00 for adults and $2.50 for children from three to twelve. Children under three are free. Children under four are not permitted in the planetarium. You'll find the museum at 524 J. Clyde Morris Boulevard in Newport News. Call (804) 595–1900.

Norfolk

Norfolk's appeal starts at its International Airport. Not necessarily architecturally gorgeous, it nevertheless offers something appealing to the soul. In other airports you're almost held captive between flights. At Norfolk, you can take a fifteen-minute walk and arrive at the enchanting paradise of the **Norfolk Botanical Gardens,** with its 175 acres of azaleas, camellias, dogwoods, roses, and other flora nestled among tall pines and placid waters, where something always is in bloom. If flowers aren't your primary interest, you can spend your between-flight time joining others as they do their daily walking and jogging exercises in beautiful surroundings. One of America's top-ten gardens, under the supervision of Robert O. Matthews, the grounds are the site of almost 200 weddings and military reenlistment ceremonies a year and the annual April International Azalea Festival. There's a $2 charge if you drive in, but it's free if you're walking from the airport. Look for the sign at the airport, or follow the road signs from Interstate 64 (804–441–5385).

The Kirn Memorial Library is the location of the Sargeant Memorial Room for historical and genealogical information. William Henry Sargeant was head librarian from 1895 until his death in 1917. He started the extensive collection of Norfolk and Virginia materials in the 1890s, and it includes census records (Virginia, 1810–1910; North Carolina, 1800–1910; and other holdings); newspapers from 1736; "how-to" books on genealogy; magazines of historical and genealogical interest; photographs of buildings, people, and places from the late 1800s to the present; early postcard scenes of Norfolk (particularly the 1907 Jamestown Exposition); Norfolk directories from 1801; assorted high school and college yearbooks from the early 1900s; and much more. All of this can help your historical and genealogical research. Of course, if you have materials such as old pictures or phone books or family histories and would like to find a safe place to keep them, the librarian will be delighted to accept your gift.

The Kirn Library is open Monday through Thursday from 9:00 A.M. to 9:00 P.M., Friday from 9:00 A.M. to 5:30 P.M. and Saturday from 9:00 A.M. to 5:00 P.M. It's at 301 East City Hall Avenue; (804) 441–2173.

Delicious eating (particularly seafood) also is a major attraction in Norfolk. An evening in this town without a visit to Joe Hoggard's Ship's Cabin is a missed opportunity. His oysters Bingo (named for local attorney Bingo Stant) and the soft-shell rock crab and Ghirardelli Square chocolate desserts are worth volumes. Ask for copies of recipes of your favorite meal. Or if you're going to be staying around for a while, check with chef Chuck

Sass, who occasionally instructs a three-hour cooking class, such as "Lite Cuisine: Seafood!" (Scallop Mousse with smoked tomato vinaigrette and cucumber lobster salsa, Thai-marinated tuna with a crispy oriental vegetable stir-fry, and peppercorn and mustard seared chicken with Vidalia-Amstel relish.) It's at 4110 East Ocean View Avenue, (804) 583-4659.

In 1912, a grand lady, the **Wells Theatre,** opened to a capacity house with Schubert's musical *The Merry Countess.* It was converted into a movie house in 1935 after the likes of Billie Burke, Douglas Fairbanks, Fred and Adele Astaire, Will Rogers, and others had trod her boards. As to other theaters of the time, the sixties brought the garish light of X-rated flicks, and a bar was built where the stage had been. The fair damsel was saved from such distress when the Virginia Stage Company took over in October 1979 and the bar was removed. The stage thrust was sent into the audience, and the lobby was returned to its approximate original size. The interior and exterior were scrubbed clean, paint applied, seats reupholstered, new carpet laid, and productions once again were mounted.

The Virginia Stage Company presents a handful of plays each year, usually worth seeing, but the amazing artistry that went into this steel-reinforced concrete structure of the pre-Beaux Arts period is a command performance. The Wells Theatre is at 108-114 East Tazewell Street. Call (804) 627-6988.

The **Chrysler Museum** was named for Walter Chrysler, Jr., in 1970 when Norfolk offered to add a wing and rename its museum for him if he would move his art collection from Provincetown, Massachusetts, to Norfolk. The city also named a concert hall at Scope for him. Long considered one of the finest galleries, the Chrysler suffered a potentially severe setback when Chrysler, the museum's chief benefactor, died and left 751 of his works to a nephew. They had been on loan to the museum, and the blow could have been devastating. The museum, however, retains more than 15,000 works (all gifts of Chrysler) in the permanent collection valued at more than $100 million. After a $13.5 million renovation and new wing project that increased the museum's space by half, the gallery had a reopening. Also unveiled at this time was the James H. Ricau collection of American neoclassical sculpture, considered the most splendid of its kind.

Mark H. Schneider, horticultural supervisor of the forty-three–acre Virginia Zoological Park, thinks it is important that exhibits be accurate, so when you visit here you will find plants in the animal exhibits and animals in the plant exhibits. With the monkeys are vines and assorted habitat plants. With the cats are jungle flora. This is such an important part of the operation that visitors receive a "Botanical Conservatory Guide" to help them through the zoo. Three special planting areas, the 4-H children's garden, Gardens for the Mentally Retarded, and Gardens for the Blind, are grouped around the conservatory, which was built in 1907. Also, there are more than 3,000 blooming annuals and 150 hanging baskets. The rose garden has beds of floribunda, hybrid tea, and climbing varieties. Zookeeper Heidi Fuciarelli notes that some of the accredited zoo's exhibits are outdated, and there's a large campaign to improve the situation. Signs of improvement include two new rare red ruffed lemurs, which recently were acquired by donation under the Species Survival Plan. The zoo is open every day except Christmas and New Year's, from 10:00 A.M. to 5:00 P.M. Admission is $2 for adults, $1 for children under twelve, and free for those under two. Free passes are issued from 4:00 P.M. to 5:00 P.M. on Sunday and Monday. The park is at 3500 Granby Street.

Northampton County

At **Etz Seafood Restaurant** in Cape Charles the food is plain but good. The crab salad in the summertime is exceptional. Neither owner George Etz nor Bonnie (the waitress) give out recipes. Soft crabs are served only April through September, and then they're out of season. Etz is normally open from 6:00 A.M. to 9:00 P.M. except Sunday. It's usually closed October and Christmas Week.

Toward the end of September you'll get caught up in Cape Charles Day, a parade and marathon with arts and crafts, clam fritters and festivities on the waterfront; for information call (804) 331–1488.

Before the time of the bridge-tunnel, there was the ferry. There's still a twenty-six-mile rail/barge ferry service running, but it's for the Eastern Shore Railroad between Cape Charles and Virginia Beach.

As you tour the Eastern Shore, you're invited to cross the Chesapeake Bay Bridge-Tunnel, the 17.6-mile link between the Eastern Shore and Virginia Beach/Norfolk, the world's longest bridge-tunnel complex. There are two mile-long tunnels, more than 12 miles of trestled railway, two bridges, nearly 2 miles of causeway, four man-made islands and 5¹/₂ miles of approach roads.

At Island 1 (the one closest to Virginia Beach), you can eat at the Sea Gull Pier restaurant, stop to watch the ships coming into and going out of the harbor, enjoy some fishing for bluefish, trout, croaker, flounder, shark and other species from the 625-foot fishing pier (bait and tackle are available), or shop at the Seashell and Gift Shop.

You might assume some interesting and perhaps life-threatening things might have happened on the bridge-tunnel, but Lorraine Smith, public relations manager for the complex, says as far as she knows, there's been only one birth (several close calls), a few medical emergencies, and nothing much else. Whether you stop to visit or go from one side to the other, it's sure a marvelous way to see the magnificent confluence of the Chesapeake Bay and the Atlantic Ocean. A forty-five–minute film about the bridge-tunnel is available for viewing by appointment.

The toll is $9 (for automobiles) each way; if, however, you tell the toll taker that you're going out to the island and will be returning without going all the way across the bay, you will be charged only once. If you don't do this ahead of time, you will be charged the second $9 toll for coming back the other direction. For further information call (804) 464–3511 (Norfolk) or (804) 331–2960 (Cape Charles).

Northumberland County

The **Sunnybank Ferry** on Route 644 has had the *Hazel* traveling between Sunnybank and Hack's Neck (near Smith Point Marina and Windmill Point) across the Little Wicomico River, or just Little River. The *Sunnybank* is another of the four ferries in Virginia, and it holds two regular-size cars or three small ones. Some 8,716 passengers were carried free across these waters in 1984. This boat has been replaced and will be set on the courthouse green. Operating hours are 7:00 A.M. to 7:00 P.M., Monday through Saturday, and there's no charge.

The *Captain Evans* is available for the memorable *Smith Island Cruise* across the scenic Chesapeake Bay to remote and historic Smith Island, Maryland (charted by Captain John Smith in 1608 and settled in 1657). Home of the Chesapeake Bay watermen, who cling to a unique and independent lifestyle, few places in America offer such undisturbed tranquility. The ninety-minute cruise leaves from the Smith Point area of Reedville, where the Potomac and Little Wicomico Rivers meet the Chesapeake Bay. Smith Island is accessible only by boat and offers a quiet retreat from fast-paced life. The island is composed of three pretty fishing villages, Ewell, Tylerton, and Rhodes Point. The 5,000-acre Glenn L. Martin Wildlife Refuge is located on the northern end of this archipelago, and the Chesapeake Bay Foundation's Field Study Center is located on Tylerton. You dock at Ewell, the largest of the three villages, for a family-style (all-you-care-to-eat) midday dinner at the Skipjack Restaurant (the meal includes crab soup, crab cakes, clam fritters, baked ham, vegetables, baked corn pudding, stewed tomatoes, cole slaw, macaroni salad, homemade hot bread with butter, beverages, homemade pie, and for additional charge, soft shell crabs). After lunch, you'll have a narrated bus tour of Ewell for a glimpse of the homes and lifestyles of the watermen, with a stop at the Tyler House, which is an exhibit of the Waterfowl Refuge. Free time is available to browse and stroll prior to boarding the *Captain Evans*. The boat ride is $16.00 and the meal is $8.50, and group rates are available. The Smith Island Cruise departs Reedville at 10:00 A.M. daily from May through mid-October and returns by 4:00 P.M. (Write Route 1, Box 289-R, Reedville 22539 or call 804-453-3430.)

Portsmouth

Virginia has an outstanding record of producing great athletes, says Herb Simpson, executive director of the **Virginia's Sports Hall of Fame.** After a look at the Texas Sports Hall of Fame in Dallas, he thought Virginia should honor its talent. So he helped organize the Hall of Fame in 1966, and in March 1972 the first induction banquet was held in Portsmouth. Its present location in Olde Towne was opened on April 3, 1977. That's where you can see uniforms, trophies, and other memorabilia highlighting the careers and records of Cy Young, Sam Snead, Arthur Ashe, Norman Snead, and Shelly Mann. Recipients must have been born in Virginia or made significant contributions to their sport(s) in Virginia. It's open Tuesday through Saturday from 10:00 A.M. to 5:00

P.M. and Sunday from 1:00 P.M. to 5:00 P.M. at 420 High Street. No admission charge; call (804) 393–8031.

While you're in Portsmouth's Olde Towne, you should take the long (one-hour) or short (fifteen-minute) walking tour along the brick sidewalks through this oldest portion of Portsmouth. Land patents were started as early as 1659. Look for Historic Portsmouth markers on streetlamps, which indicate stopping points.

Along the way you'll see the Cassell House, with its hand-carved arched doorway and stone lintels and sills at the window; the Old Courthouse, built in 1846; Trinity Church, the oldest church in Portsmouth, dating back to 1761; and numerous other buildings that represent a variety of architectural styles and influences including Dutch colonial, English basement, Gothic Revival, Victorian, Federal and Romanesque Revival.

Additional information about Portsmouth's architecture is available for a slight charge at the Office of City Planning, One High Street. The walking brochure is free; call (804) 393–8836.

Virginia Beach

The Virginia Beach WPA mural in the post office on Atlantic Avenue and 24th Street is a 1939 piece by John H. R. Pickett entitled *Old Dominion Conversation Piece,* about tobacco and settlers. It's quite dark (except where some recent wall paint has splashed upon it) and probably could use a cleaning. (We're sure the others we've mentioned could as well, and we've heard there is a statewide plan to refurbish these paintings, which pleases us greatly.)

Virginia Beach is noted for its **Mt. Trashmore,** which solved two major problems in this community. First, it provided a place for a solid waste landfill. Instead of filling shallow holes (high water table), it built a mountain. Second, it provided a large recreational facility, which includes a soapbox derby run, for which you need a hill, and hills, to say the least, aren't too plentiful in this oceanside community. Kite flying is a trip in the spring, and on a brisk March day the air is filled with colorful boxes and other flights of fancy. Without fear of contradiction, Mt. Trashmore was an inspiration for dozens of other cities in this country and other countries as a solution for solid waste and recreational problems. Mt. Trashmore will be on your right as you drive from Interstate 64 to Virginia Beach on the expressway.

You can see Arabian horses at the **Cashvan's Horse Farm** on 2352 Princess Anne Road in Virginia Beach. Free tours are available by appointment Tuesday through Sunday, from 1:00 P.M. to 4:00 P.M. Photos are not allowed, and you're requested not to pet the horses. Shows and exhibitions are conducted at Cashvan, which is managed by Hy Cashvan and Jay Wilks, and their horses compete in other shows. They run an extensive breeding facility, and Cashvan and Wilkes recently donated two Arabians to Virginia Beach for the city's beach patrol. For more information call (804) 427–5316.

The **Old Cape Henry Lighthouse,** authorized and funded by America's first Congress, was built in 1791 and was the first public building authorized by that body. This lighthouse, near the entrance to the Chesapeake Bay, was used for almost ninety years, until 1881. The stones were mined in the Aquia Quarries, which also provided stone for the Capitol building, the White House, and Mount Vernon. It's open from mid-May to November 1, and for a small admission charge you can visit inside. Enter through the Fort Story gate, off Route 60. Call (804) 460–1688.

It was off Cape Henry that the ships of Admiral Francois Joseph Paul Comte de Grasse, while the land side was blocked by the Franco-American armies of Washington, Rochambeau and Lafayette, prevented action by Gen. Lord Cornwallis and led to his surrender to Washington on October 19, 1781. This little-mentioned skirmish apparently had no victor, but it allowed the Americans time to bring up their heavy siege guns, which marked the beginning of the end of the war. A statue of Admiral de Grasse, a gift from France, is also located at Fort Story in Virginia Beach, withing sight of the Old Cape Henry Lighthouse.

If the weather permits, the Virginia Beach Farmers Market is open every day of the year at 1989 Landstown Road. There are 17,000 square feet of vendors' stalls where you can buy fresh produce, baked goods, meats, dairy products, seafood, and plants.

"Is there gold in seawater?" "How do waves change our coastline?" "What is it like beneath the surface of the Chesapeake Bay?" The answers to these questions and more are waiting to be discovered at the **Virginia Marine Science Museum.** From the "Journey of Water" section, which features a walk through the Coastal Plains River habitat and an outside boardwalk loop to view the many creatures that live in this tidal environment, to the Chesapeake Bay Hall to the Man and Marine Environment, this museum should be able to answer any question you have ever had about this tidewater area. From a 50,000-gallon aquarium to artifacts of early Indian inhabitants of the Chesapeake Bay area, the Virginia Marine Science Museum has tried to anticipate your every wish and interest.

Open from 9:00 A.M. to 9:00 P.M. Monday through Saturday and 9:00 A.M. to 5:00 P.M. Sunday, from June through early September; 9:00 A.M. to 5:00 P.M. daily from September through May. Adults are $3.25; children 12 and under and senior citizens 62 and over are $2.50. Write 717 General Booth Boulevard, Virginia Beach, 23451 or call (804) 425–FISH.

For those interested in a quality micro-brewery product, available only in the Virginia and Washington, D.C., area, you have Johnathan Miller to thank. Miller has purchased the former Chesapeake Bay Brewery in Virginia Beach and renamed it the **Virginia Brewing Company.** The Chesbay labels are gone and the Doppelbock labels are here. Actual brewing chores are handled by a Bavarian-born brewmeister, Wolfgang Roth, with the distribution and placement and business end handled by Miller. You'll find the brew at such places as the several Clyde's restaurants, the Occidental Restaurant in Washington, and Union Street Public House in Old Town Alexandria. Miller is the third owner of this brewery in three years. His plans will take it from producing 2,400 barrels a year to a more stable and profitable 20,000 barrels.

Williamsburg

Colonial Williamsburg, the restored portion of Williamsburg, has a new visitor center acting as the gateway to the colonial triangle. New traffic patterns have been established, and new audiovisuals, information kiosks, ticket windows (up to fourteen during busy times) and other aids to assist tourists have been added. You'll still be invited to see *Williamsburg—The Story of a Patriot,* and then dual escalators and a stairway will allow you to go from the main floor to the enlarged bus lobby.

There are plenty of books and pamphlets available (some free, some not). Two new features opened in Colonial Williamsburg (CW) in 1985. The Public Hospital of 1773, on its original foundations near the southeast corner of Francis and Henry streets, was the largest and last reconstruction project undertaken by CW since 1934 when the Governor's Palace and the Capitol were finished. From the hospital, walk through the underground walkway to the new DeWitt Wallace Decorative Arts Gallery, which exhibits a wide range of eighteenth-century artifacts from Colonial Williamsburg's private collection. The display includes paintings, textiles, needlework, and more items that had been sitting around with no room in which to be displayed.

Not everything in CW is handicapped accessible (accessible buildings were not necessarily a prime architectural concern in the eighteenth and nineteenth centuries), but the Colonial Williamsburg Foundation is eager to make you feel as welcome as possible and to assist you as much as they can. Some places are accessible, some places have portable wheelchair ramps available, and slide programs about inaccessible areas of some of the buildings are being created. On the other hand, there are few curbs in the restored city, and automobiles are not permitted on the main streets during the day. An escorted walking tour is available for the visually impaired, and a special tour of the Powell-Waller House can be arranged. Free publications for the hearing impaired are available, including a printed synopsis of *The Story of a Patriot,* for which special head sets may also be used. Several interpreters are available, as are discount tickets for some programs. Write or ask for a copy of the Colonial Williamsburg *Guide for the Handicapped* at P.O. Box C, Williamsburg 23187; (804) 229–1000.

York County

The **Yorktown Shipwreck Archaeological Project,** under the direction of John Broadwater, is excavating an eighteenth-century British merchant ship believed to be part of Gen. Charles Cornwallis's fleet, which he had sunk at the end of the Revolutionary War. These shipwrecks are on the Historic Register—the first underwater site to be so designated. A metal cofferdam constructed around the wreck and lined with a white plastic material keeps the water clear so workers can see up to about 20 feet and so visitors can see the workers. They're hoping to stop some of the leakage of seawater into the cofferdam so visibility will be even better. Broadwater (who was first mate on the Atlantic voyage of the replica *Godspeed* during the summer of 1985) says they do not plan to bring up the ship but are looking to learn about shipboard life two centuries ago.

The project is at the foot of Comte de Grasse Street, and there's a pier out to the ship and cofferdam so you can observe the activities, which take place from the end of May through the end of October. A videotape presentation is now available. There is an admission charge for the guided tour. If you'd like to receive a free newsletter about the Yorktown Shipwreck Archaeological Project (YSAP), write to the Ship Committee, P.O. Box 2016, Yorktown 23690 or call (804) 898–0002.

A visit to Yorktown certainly isn't a visit without a stop at **Nick's Seafood Pavilion,** started by Nick and Mary Matthews, wonderful people who came from Greece in the 1950s. The restaurant is located on the site where British General Cornwallis surrendered to George Washington on October 19, 1781. The Matthewses became so involved with the community that they donated the land where the Yorktown Victory Center is located. There's an exhibit in the center about the Matthewses, as examples of the great American dream come true. Nick passed away several years ago, but Mary continues the grand tradition of good food and an unusual atmosphere (the interior is filled with statues of gods and goddesses, plants, and mosaics made in Italy). The doors open at 11:00 A.M. Follow the signs (and the aromas) as you cross the York River Bridge. Nick's phone number is (804) 887–5269.

When restoration and reconstruction take place in many historic sites, it's often done behind drapes, fences, or other barricades. That's no longer the case at **Jamestown Festival Park.** Bill Hancock, exhibit maintenance supervisor, and his carpenters now do their repair work in period costumes, with reproduction seventeenth-century tools, as part of the interpretive program. They're delighted to answer your questions. A new indoor museum complex will open in late 1989, at which time the Festival Park's name will change to Jamestown Settlement. Admission is $5 for adults and $2.50 for children six through twelve. For additional information, contact the Jamestown-Yorktown Foundation, P.O. Drawer JF, in Williamsburg; (804) 253–4838.

Off the Beaten Path in Central-Southside Virginia

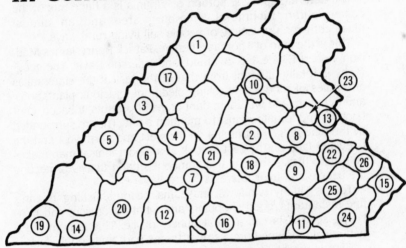

1. Albemarle County
   Boar's Head Inn
   Hatton Ferry
2. Amelia County
   Sayler's Creek
3. Amherst County
   Amherst County Historical Museum
4. Appomattox County
5. Bedford County
   Bedford Museum
6. Campbell County
   Lane Furniture Company
7. Charlotte County
   Red Hill Shrine
8. Chesterfield County
   Chesterfield County Museum
9. Dinwiddie County
10. Goochland County
    Fox Head Inn
11. Greensville County
    Virginia Peanut Festival
12. Halifax County
    South Boston Historical Museum
13. Henrico County
    Best Products corporate
       headquarters
    Virginia Aviation Museum
    Barksdale Theatre
14. Henry County
    Virginia Museum of Natural History
15. Isle of Wight County
    St. Luke's Church

16. Mecklenburg County
    Buggs Island Lake
17. Nelson County
    Schuyler
18. Nottoway County
    Armbruster's Restaurant
19. Patrick County
20. Pittsylvania County
    Tobacco and Textile Museum
    Pittsylvania County Museum
21. Prince Edward County
    Reverend E. Francis Griffin
       monument
22. Prince George County
    Blandford Church and Cemetery
    Siege Museum
    U.S. Army Quartermaster Museum
    Flowerdew Hundred
23. Richmond
    Capitol
    Lewis Ginter Botanical Garden
    Phillip Morris manufacturing plant
    Science Museum of Virginia
    Bensonhouse of Richmond
    Jefferson Hotel
24. Sussex County
    Virginia Diner
25. Surry County
    Bacon's Castle
    Scotland-Jamestown Ferry

Central-Southside Virginia

The Central-Southside portion of Virginia is a huge mix of the cosmopolitan Richmond-Petersburg area and an almost nineteenth-century feeling of people still living rural ways.

This is the land of Thomas Jefferson, Patrick Henry, James Madison, Robert E. Lee, J. E. B. Stuart, and Jefferson Davis. The geography is totally different from that of the rest of the state: miles and miles of moderately rolling piedmont; gracious plantations; and rich farmland with abundant crops of peanuts, tobacco, cantaloupe, and tomatoes, just to mention a few. They're surrounded by the Blue Ridge Mountains on the west and northwest and the tidewater land on the east. A look at a topographical map makes you think this is the palm of someone's hand that is protecting the people and their interests.

This is Tiffany windows, museums, peanuts, fishing, boating, fine restaurants, good shopping, and what advertisers and marketing specialists call a great quality of life. This is home to a nationally renowned amusement theme park and county fairs.

Here is where Fortune 500 companies have and are locating and where you can find "the world's best homemade apple butter." It's home on Millionaires' Row and tobacco auctioneer competitions. This is Lake Gaston and Buggs Island and great fishing and boating and vacation homes and small-town celebrations and festivals.

Listen a little and you'll hear of buried treasure and the largest variety of mineral stones in the state, quill pens made for the United States Supreme Court, hot-air balloon rides, an incredible variety of architectural styles, and the home of Earl Hamner, Jr., of Walton's Mountain fame.

Albemarle County

Charlottesville is the home of Thomas Jefferson's Monticello, the University of Virginia, and so much more; but you should begin your visit here with the Western Virginia Bicentennial Center. First, it's in a lovely setting, particularly in the fall. Second, an interesting exhibit shows the life of Jefferson and Virginians in

Jefferson's time. Third, you can buy admission tickets to Monticello and receive an up-to-the-minute estimate of how long the wait is to visit Jefferson's home. It may be the only information center for which you should allow an hour for your visit (because of the exhibit). The Bicentennial Center is open from 9:00 A.M. to 5:30 P.M. from March 1 through October 31 and 9:00 A.M. to 5:00 P.M. November 1 through February 28; closed Thanksgiving, Christmas, and New Year's Day. You can talk with Barbara Cochran and the staff. It's on Route 20, south of Interstate 64; (804) 893–6789.

You can take a walking tour of Historic Downtown Charlottesville along the pedestrian mall. There's a Victorian hardware store from 1909 (now a restaurant and shopping gallery), a Smith's of Bermuda shop, the Paramount Theater (1931), one of three identical theaters (the other two, in Newport News and Lynchburg, have been destroyed), and other places of note.

Also along the pedestrian mall you'll find the Goose Quill Pen shop where Lewis "Quill" Glaser handmade goose quill pens for thirty-six years. He sent 700 pens to the U.S. Supreme Court every fall for the first Monday in October opening of that judicial body. You can have a set of two Glaser pens in a John Marshall pewter inkstand for $25, plus $5 for engraving and $3 for postage. Stop by the upstairs store at 107 West Main Street in Historic Downtown Charlottesville; (804) 293–8531.

The Boar's Head Inn in Charlottesville is relatively new facility (1965), but it has old ties. John B. Rogan purchased an 1834 waterwheel gristmill that had been built on a stretch of the Hardware River by Martin Thacker and Martin Dawson. Saved from Civil War destruction, it was operated for sixty years by R. J. Hancock. When Rogan purchased the mill in the early 1960s, he had it dismantled, numbered the pieces, and had it reconstructed on the Boar's Head Inn property. Fieldstones from the mill's original foundation were used in the inn's fireplace and in the arched stone entrance below the ordinary. The heartwood pine beams, which form the structure, are as long as 43 feet. The flooring is the old pine planking from the mill, still bearing the scars of barrels once rolled across its surface. Lumber from the former grain bins was redressed for panelling in the Old Mill Room and the ordinary. The blue boar's head was a symbol of hospitality in Elizabethan England well translated at this Boar's Head Inn.

Available at the inn are three indoor Grasstex tennis courts, ten Lee Fast-Dry clay courts, three platform tennis courts and four squash courts, pools, a health club, fishing in one of the lakes on the property, and gorgeous grounds through which you can stroll. Call (804) 296-2181.

Of special note are the Bear Balloon Corporation's balloon flights, run from the Boar's Head by Rick Behr, a full-time professional balloonist since 1974 with over 3,000 hours of hot-air ballooning. Prior to coming to the Boar's Head, he was chief pilot of the Chalet Club in New York and then on Buddy Bombard's Great French Balloon Adventure.

Rick will give you the ride of your life over the beautiful mountains and rolling countryside. He says he has the largest passenger balloons in the country, and he can take about ten passengers on each flight. He works with groups of twenty people, taking ten on the flight and ten in a chase vehicle where you can take pictures of the balloon ascending or descending or just flying, and then switching everyone, so the first ten can take pictures and the second ten can go flying.

Flights are scheduled for shortly after dawn and shortly before dusk, April through November, and of course each flight is finished with the traditional bottle of champagne. Even those who are afraid of heights and flying enjoy this marvelous experience. The cost is $100 per person on weekdays for a forty-five–minute flight and $125 per person on weekends for flights of sixty to seventy-five minutes. Times are always approximate, and flights go only if weather conditions permit. These flights probably are the least expensive balloon rides in the country. Group balloon programs may be arranged. You don't have to be a guest at the Boar's Head to ride. Call (804) 296-2181, ext. 2146.

The Boar's Head Inn Store (804-295-0525) opened in the fall of 1985 during the annual wine festival. Elinor Larkin, the manager, is building up her collection of Virginia-made products, such as wines and foodstuffs, and it should be an interesting and convenient place to shop.

Micro-breweries are becoming popular across the country, and Charlottesville has one of its own. The Blue Ridge Restaurant & Brewing Co. is so small that at the moment it only produces enough suds to serve in the pub. Brothers Paul and Bok Summers (grandsons of William Faulkner) have opened this self-contained, comfortable, and casual neighborhood watering place. Local products, such as Virginia wines, Afton Ale and Hawksbill Golden Lager, Virginia hams, apples, and peaches all flavor or provide the basis for the menu. Lunch is available from 11:30 A.M. to 2:00 P.M. Tuesday through Friday, brunch from 11:30 A.M. to 3:00 P.M. weekends, and dinner from 5:00 P.M. to 10:00 P.M. Tuesday through Saturday. The pub is open during the in-between hours but closed on Monday. You'll find it at 709 West Main Street; (804) 977–0017.

A little farther south on Route 20 is Scottsville, situated at the northernmost point of the James River, where you can find a row of Federal-style stores on Valley Street, a tobacco warehouse, and other structures built in the early 1800s. The James River and Kanawha Canal was built here in the nineteenth century, and Scottsville (originally the county seat) was the first important stop after Richmond. A ferry served Scottsville and the residents across the river, but where it docked on the other side was private property. So, according to legend, the ferry was moved several miles upstream to settle or prevent a lawsuit.

The **Hatton Ferry** still operates on weekends if the water is high enough. It's called a pole ferry, even though it's rigged with ropes and winches. When the rope is played out on one side, the tide swings the boat around and carries it across the river, and then the process is reversed; but it still needs poling to berth it securely. To take the ferry, drive west on Route 6, following the signs for the ferry or the James River Runners.

Just up the hill from the Hatton ferry (you have to pass them to get to the ferry) are the offices of the James River Runners, Inc. Jeff and Christie Schmick provide canoes, inner tubes, floating islands, a shuttle service, and almost anything else you need to go down the James River in style. You should provide your own lunch and bring another change of clothes. They recommend that you wear wool for early spring and fall canoeing, and bring suntan lotion, sunglasses or a hat, but don't take anything onto the river that you don't want to get wet or can't afford to lose.

Canoe and rafting rates run from $10 for 3-mile trip to $29 per person for an overnight trip. Tubing trips (they say they're the largest tubing operation on the James River) are $8 per person for tube and transportation. Christie says you don't have to be experienced, just eager to enjoy the beautiful scenery available to you during your leisurely trip. Reservations are strongly recommended, although last-minute accommodations can be handled sometimes. Credit cards are not accepted. Jeff says they change the canoes every year or two, which means that you'll be getting good, new equipment and also that you might want to check with them in the fall if you're thinking of buying a canoe. The Runners are located off Route 6, west of Route 20 and south of Charlottesville; (804) 286–2338.

Amelia County

The last major battle of the Civil War was fought in Amelia County, at **Sayler's Creek,** and the Battlefield Historical State Park commemorates the Confederate Army's crippling defeat on April 6, 1865, which led to General Lee's surrender at Appomattox seventy-two hours later. Reenactments are held here on the Sunday closest to April 6 unless that's an Easter Sunday, when the re-creation is held the following Sunday. There's a nice genealogical library and a small museum open on Monday, Wednesday, and Friday from 10:00 A.M. to 4:00 P.M.

Amherst County

The **Amherst County Historical Museum** was built in 1891 as the second county jail, complete with an iron plate interior for security. It was replaced in the 1930s when the new jail was built next door, and most of the metal was stripped for World War II production. Two of the old jail's cells remain, and the museum houses county history going back to the early woodland Indians, with fragments of a 3,000-year-old Indian soapstone bowl, Sir Jeffery Amherst's original coat of arms, and Civil War money. Slide lectures are available. The jail became a museum in 1974 as part of our country's bicentennial celebration. The museum is open Tuesday through Saturday from 9:30 A.M. to noon and 1:00 P.M. to 5:00 P.M. There's no admission charge. It's on Taylor Street on the Courthouse Square. Follow the signs from Route 29; (804) 946–9348.

Appomattox County

Appomattox is the site of the surrender of Gen. Robert E. Lee to Gen. Ulysses S. Grant on April 9, 1865, which ended the Civil War; on a lighter note, it is also the birthplace of Joe Sweeney, originator of the five-string banjo. You can stop by Appomattox in mid-October for the annual Railroad Festival started in 1973. Billed as an event to promote Historic Appomattox and the contributions the railroad made to the area, of course the two-day festival is to be enjoyed. You can see Civil War memorabilia and miniature trains, participate in the Joe Sweeney Classic (a 10-K race), enjoy country cooking at the depot (which survived the war, but succumbed to fire in 1923 and was rebuilt by Norfolk and Western in 1924), take a carnival ride, fly in a helicopter, watch a chain saw competition, and, of course, see fireworks.

Bedford County

The Peaks of Otter overlook Bedford, "The World's Best Little Town" (population 6,000), as you enter a western approach to the part of the state called Southside. Before entering the town, you can take a hike up the 3,875-foot high Sharp Top, said by Bedford residents to be Virginia's most famous mountain. A stone from the top of Sharp Top was Virginia's contribution to the Washington Monument in 1852.

In the middle of the Bedford City Historical District is the **Bedford Museum,** housed in the 1895 Masonic building on Main Street since 1979. It features two floors of displays, including old photographs, surgical instruments, a 100-year-old wedding dress worn by Miss Anspaugh, daughter of Col. David Anspaugh, and a Benjamin Franklin printing press used at the Bedford *Bulletin.* The only other press like it is at the Smithsonian Institution in Washington.

The museum's library of historical and genealogical materials is well used by those trying to find their family histories. Special lectures and films are shown in the evening. The library also has a file on the legendary hidden Beale's treasure. There are some who say a treasure was buried in a cave near Montvale by a party of adventurers who returned from a trip to the west laden with gold and other valuables "long years prior to the War Between the States." Others say the treasure's been recovered, while others say there wasn't any treasure in the first place. The directions to the treasure were left in a sealed box in a Lynchburg bank. When the box was opened there were three intricate codes describing the treasure and its location. Reportedly, two of the codes have been deciphered, but so far no one seems to have broken the third code. You can come to your own conclusion after looking at the file and checking the maps.

Admission to the museum is $1 for adults and 50¢ for children. It's open Tuesday through Saturday, 10:00 A.M. to 5:00 P.M. Call (703) 586–4520. The museum is closed January and February.

If you'd like to talk to some of the older residents of the county, visit the folks at the Elks National Home, where you can swap stories about Beale's treasure. This has been the national retirement home of the Fraternal Order of Elks since 1903. Sitting on 180 acres, the biggest attraction is the Christmas lighting (thousands and thousands of light bulbs) that draws visitors from hundreds of miles around and gives Bedford its other title, "Christmas Capital of Virginia."

For more details on things to do in Bedford, stop by the Chamber of Commerce and Information Center on Main Street and talk to John Mitchell. Check the pictures of the Fireman's Band. They've been to several presidential inaugurations and the Macy's Thanksgiving Day Parades. There's even one picture of the original band. The office is closed from noon to 1:00 P.M. weekdays.

Campbell County

In 1940, Herman Maril painted the mural *The Growing Community* in the Altavista Post Office on Bedford Avenue and Seventh Street. It depicts the train station on the right and the Lane Furniture factory on the left. The Lane Furniture Company was started in 1907 by John Edward Lane when he bought a box plant for $500. That box plant has grown into a company with nineteen plants in four states covering ninety-two acres of floor space and employing over 5,000 people. The company developed the first known moving conveyor assembly system in the furniture industry during World War I and became known through advertising in such national publications as the *Saturday Evening Post* and the "girl graduate program," which has given miniature cedar chests to some 15,000,000 high school girl graduates since 1930. If, as a female graduate, you grew up in an area that didn't have a store sponsoring the cedar chest program, or if you want another chest, you can purchase the miniature chests here.

Altavista, we were told, was named for a farm owned by Henry Lane. Be sure to stay away from the plant around 3:30 P.M. when the shift lets out. Group tours sometimes are available (for classes) by writing ahead of time to Richard K. McKeel, Lane Furniture Co., Inc., P.O. Box 191, Altavista 24517.

The first Saturday of each month buyers and sellers from as far away as California and Florida are attracted to the "trade lot" for one of the country's oldest flea markets, an Altavista tradition started in 1919. It's held on Seventh Street, "right in the middle of town," says Mrs. Sarah F. Simpson of the Altavista Chamber of Commerce, and it now starts as early as noon on Friday and runs until it closes down on Saturday.

Crossing over Seneca Creek is the oldest covered bridge still standing in Virginia. It's a 26-foot span built in 1878 and used until 1952, when it was replaced by a more modern structure built alongside it. There's a catwalk from a small wayside area to the bridge, known locally as the Marysville Bridge. Travel south 3.3 miles on Route 761 from Highway 501 at Gladys to Route 705. Turn right and continue about 1 1/2 miles.

Charlotte County

The **Red Hill Shrine** was Patrick Henry's last home and burial place. One of seven different homes he had, this was said to be his favorite as "one of the garden spots of the world." It's the home of the nation's oldest osage orange tree, with a span of ninety feet and height of fifty-four feet. It's estimated to be 350 to 400 years old. Red Hill Shrine is open daily from 9:00 A.M. to 5:00 P.M. April 1 through October 31 and 9:00 A.M. to 4:00 P.M. the rest of the year. Admission is $3 for adults, $2 for senior citizens, and $1 for students and children. Red Hill Shrine is at Route 2 in Brookneal; to get there, drive 5 miles east of Brookneal on Route 600. Call (804) 376–2044 for more information.

Chesterfield County

The **Chesterfield County Museum** in Chesterfield was started by the Ruritan Clubs of the county in the early 1950s. It features a reproduction of the original 1750 Chesterfield County

Courthouse, the story of Chesterfield presented through narration and artifacts, a replica of an old-fashioned country store, the 1892 jail (in service through 1962), and on the green, monuments to Baptist ministers imprisoned in 1773 and to Confederate soldiers. It's toward the back of the Courthouse Green, off Route 10 west of Interstate 95. Visiting hours are 10:00 A.M. to 4:00 P.M. Tuesday through Friday and 1:00 P.M. to 5:00 P.M. on Sunday. Suggested donations are $1 for adults and 50¢ for children; (804) 748–1026.

Across the Court Green is the Magnolia Grange museum house. Built in 1822, the house is one of the finest examples of Federal-period architecture in Virginia and is appropriately furnished. Visiting hours are 10:00 A.M. to 4:00 P.M. Tuesday through Friday and 1:00 P.M. to 5:00 P.M. on Sunday. Admission fee is $2 for adults, $1.50 for senior citizens, and $1 for students. Contributions, as well as reservations for tours, may be sent to Magnolia Grange, Chesterfield Historical Society, P.O. Box 40, Chesterfield 23832.

To the northwest of Petersburg is Colonial Heights, home of Violet Bank, a spreading cucumber tree, and Lee's headquarters for five months beginning June 8, 1864 (he had to leave when the falling leaves bared his position). The name Violet Bank seems to have come from the profusion of violets growing on the hillside. The Civil War Museum there boasts of an autographed photo of "Stonewall" Jackson and other items of interest to Civil War buffs. The Colonial Heights Federated Woman's Club is responsible for the restoration of the ornamented ceilings and reproduction furniture from a period around 1815. The cucumber tree, or *Magnolia acuminata,* seems to date back to Jefferson's time. It's noted for being the second largest in the country and for being out of place, for the tree rarely grows east of the Blue Ridge.

From April 1 through October 31, the museum is open 10:00 A.M. to 3:00 P.M. weekdays, except on Thursday, and Sunday from 1:00 P.M. to 5:00 P.M. It's at 303 Virginia Avenue, one block off Route 1/301 in Colonial Heights; (804) 520–4244.

Dinwiddie County

As you travel along Highway 1 through Dinwiddie, you're likely to be surprised at the condition of this former main thoroughfare.

Replaced in late 1960s by Interstate 85, the road is three lanes wide with the center lane reserved for passing and left turns. Grass grows in the cracks of this once mighty lifeline of the north-south route. There is little construction along the route; few inns or watering spots dot its shoulders. There are almost no neon signs trying to allure passerby, as you'll see further north. It's silent testimony to the way things were.

Goochland County

Phillip, Barbara, and Scott Pettit, the innkeepers of the **Fox Head Inn** in Manakin-Sabot, are hosts and hostess supreme, and the food is equally outstanding. Epicurean delight is an understatement. House specialties include a lobster and shrimp casserole, aged western steaks, and country fried chicken, but our favorite probably is the crab cake. After you've tasted one of the desserts, you may think they should be served first to make sure you have enough room for one. Featured on the dessert menu are fox hunter pie (nuts and chocolate bits topped with whipped cream), hot apple cobbler, huntsman's cheesecake, and other daily offerings.

In the middle of fox-hunting country the farmhouse is turn-of-the-century preserved to perfection and has been operated by the Pettits (former caterers) since 1971. The converted gaslight chandelier in the entrance hall originally was in the home of the Gwaltneys of Smithfield fame. The buggy wheel light served as a wheel before its current occupation. The fox head theme is carried out with twin brass fox head door knockers, a brass fox head on the newel post, and a real fox head mounted on the wall. The rooms are set in country kitchen, tobacco, hunt, and thoroughbred motifs, and the atmosphere is low-key, folksy, and intimate. Upstairs you might find a miniature house Phillip and Barbara are building.

The Fox Head is open at 6:30 P.M. every evening except Sunday. Last diners are accepted at 8:00 P.M. The inn is about thirty minutes out of Richmond out Patterson Avenue, north to Route 623, left on Route 621. The inn will be on your left. Or, take the Manakin exit off Interstate 64, taking Route 623 south 1.2 miles to a right turn onto Route 250, then to Route 621. Call (804) 784–5126.

Greensville County

The Greensville County–Emporia area sponsored the twenty-third annual Virginia Peanut Festival in 1985 with beauty pageants, a cocktail party, breakfast in the park, farm tours, an arts and craft show, entertainment, a parade, a dance, a chicken barbecue dinner, and a Virginia Peanut Cooking Contest. Call (804) 634–6095 for information on this year's festival. (Check Southampton County for more peanut talk.)

Andree Ruellen created the 1941 WPA post office mural *Country Sawmill* at 109 South Main Street, Emporia. The sawmill depicts a real one belonging to the Daughtry and Davis Sawmill, which was replaced by a shopping center. If you can find J. R. Pritchard, retired postmaster, he can tell you who all the people are in the painting. The original 1938 safe from York Safe and Lock Company of York, Pennsylvania, is still used in the post office.

Halifax County

Halifax County is the third largest in the state. Its land is level to gently rolling and is filled with tobacco (Halifax County was for many years the largest tobacco-producing county in the country), commercial forests (the state's largest agricultural revenue producer), and large tracts of apparently endless land. At one time, there were 4,000 active farms, most of them small. Now there are also factories representing companies such as Westinghouse, J. P. Stevens, Burlington, Champion International, Daystrom Furniture, Sale Knitting, Wabash Magnetics, Craddock-Terry Shoe Corporation, C. K. Company, Vulcan Materials, Presto Products, Clover Yarns, Rochester Button, South Boston Manufacturing, and Switzer Furniture.

As an alternative means of funding, the Halifax County Chamber of Commerce started an annual Turbeville Cantaloupe Festival in 1981. The festival is held the fourth Wednesday of each July on John Wade's farm 9 miles west of South Boston on Route 58. Cantaloupe was chosen because it's patented, only seven people grow it (Wade is one of them), it can only be grown in this rich chocolate brown soil (Wickham) in a narrow strip of land along the Dan River, and cantaloupe grown here are much larger and much sweeter than other cantaloupe. Although the festival technically runs from 4:00 P.M. to 9:00 P.M., the action starts much earlier as some 3,200 pounds of sirloin tip roasts are brought in and placed in 6-foot pits where wood has been burning down to coals for twelve hours. Eight hours later the barbecue beef is ready for serving, along with about 24 bushels of tomatoes, 9,000 ears of corn, 400 packages of dinner rolls, about 2,000 cantaloupe (picked fresh that morning), and bluegrass music. It's much like a "big old homecoming," says the Chamber of Commerce's Nancy Pool. All you have to bring is your appetite, your lawn chair, and the cost of admission, which is under $10.

Cantaloupe is so delicious by itself that it seems logical it would make other foods taste even better. So, a cantaloupe cut-up recipe contest was held in 1985 that brought in recipes for melon with chicken, melon franks (slit a hot dog and stuff with a slice of melon, wrap with bacon, and secure with a toothpick before roasting on the grill), cantaloupe pancakes, melon with chablis or piña colada mix, and cantaloupe preserves. For more information, call (804) 572–3085.

On North Main Street in South Boston, you'll find one of 139 Constitution oak trees given to members of the state's Constitutional Convention of 1901–02. The oaks were distributed throughout the state in 1902 as "living memorials" to the convention. Joseph Stebbins, Sr., was one of two delegates from Halifax County. His tree, at what is now the home of Mr. and Mrs. Edward Albright, is one of perhaps two dozen known to be still living throughout the entire state.

At North Main Street and Wilborn Avenue is the Obituary Pole, where notices of deaths and funerals have been posted since this century was in its teens. It's said the practice started when Mr. Owen, of the J. S. Owen Funeral Home, tired of people coming into the home asking about funerals and started posting the notices on a corner pole to resolve the problem.

With so much history here (the county seat dates back to 1777 and two military campaigns—the Retreat to the Dan in the Revolutionary War and the Battle of Staunton River in the Civil War—culminated or occurred in Halifax County), it's natural to have a historical museum. The Tuesday Women's Club established the **South Boston Historical Museum** in 1982, which houses the permanent collections and loans of items relating to Halifax. The first buggy ever made by a nationally known local company is on display at the museum. The museum is open from 9:00 A.M. to 4:00 P.M. on Thursday and Friday and 2:00 P.M. to 4:30 P.M. on Sunday. The building is on Yancey street (parelleling Broad), past the post office, off Fenton; (804) 572–9200.

Henrico County

The **Best Products corporate headquarters** also is headquarters for an extensive interior and exterior art collection. Greeting you on the exterior are diamond-patterned glass blocks in pale turquoise, fountains, and two 1939 art deco eagles from the Airlines Terminal Building of New York. Inside, you'll find a water lily carpet pattern adapted from a Jack Beal silkscreen, Andy Warhol pieces, and other diverse elements taken from architectural styles from the Renaissance to exposed mechanical systems, spanning more than 600 years of art history. It's pleasure to see art and architecture blend so beautifully and inspirationally with everyday life. The lobby area is open during normal working hours. More extensive tours can be arranged by calling Dean Jarrett in Corporate Communications. Best is at 954 North Parham Road, off Interstate 95, just north of Richmond; (804) 261–2378.

As mentioned in the first edition of *Virginia: Off the Beaten Path*, the Shannon collection of airplanes from the Fredericksburg area was scheduled to be moved to a new museum site. And so it has. The **Virginia Aviation Museum,** located at the Richmond International Airport, offers you an hour's walk through aviation history. Here you can see Captain Dick Merrill's 1930s open-cockpit mail plane, examine aircraft engines from the pioneering days (aviation pioneering, not Daniel Boone pioneering), take a memorable close look at a World War I SPAD, stroll past exhibits of aviation artifacts, and see the special exhibit dedicated to Virginia's legendary Admiral Richard E. Byrd. Check with curator Bill Kennedy if you have any special questions or need information about special programs. A small gift shop is open in the lobby. This is a project of the Virginia Aeronautical Historical Society and is open from 10:00 A.M. to 4:00 P.M. Tuesday through Saturday and 10:00 A.M. to 4:00 P.M. on Sunday from April 1 through September 30, and from 1:00 P.M. to 5:00 P.M. October 1 to March 31. It is closed Monday and major holidays. The address is 5701 Huntsman Road, Sandston and the phone number is (804) 222–8690.

Nancy Kilgore is one of the founders of **Barksdale Theatre,** and she tells this tale: "On August 1, 1953, six actors, two children, a dog, cat, and two pigs moved into a historic ruin called Hanover Tavern, determined to make it their personal home and a professional theater. They had youth, enthusiasm, and a name: Barksdale Memorial Theatre, honoring a Charlottesville girl, Barbara Barksdale, a college friend who had died of multiple sclerosis." Keeping full-time jobs to pay the mortgage, they began drumming up theater business in the tiny community of Hanover Court House. They found that Hanover clubs wanted to dine out on group excursions, so they were soon cooking and waiting tables to lure audiences to private performances. Thus was hatched the nation's first dinner theater, though Barksdale prefers to be known as a theater that happens to have a restaurant, and dinner is optional.

They've been going strong ever since, receiving high praise for the play selection and presentation. You, too, can enjoy the fine menu in one of five candle-lit rooms, have Nancy take you on a historic tour of the courthouse, the jail, and the 1723 tavern and stagecoach stop, and see marvelous theater. Performances are given Wednesday through Saturday at 8:30 P.M. For show only, prices are $10 Wednesday and Thursday, $11 Friday, and $12 Saturday; add $12 for dinner. There are some special rates available for groups, students, and seniors. Call (804) 537–5333 or write to the Barksdale Theatre, Box 7, Hanover 23069.

Henry County

One of the newest museums in the state is the **Virginia Museum of Natural History** in Martinsville, under the direction of Drs. Noel T. and Dorothy Boaz. Oceanography (mainly an exhibit of shells) and astronomy (mainly planets) are the subjects of the two permanent displays. Other exhibits rotate and might cover dinosaurs (the opening exhibit), American Indian heritage, rocks and minerals, holography, Ice Age Virginia, African explorations, botany, insects, rivers and streams, and reptiles and amphibians. There is a gift shop. The museum is located at 1001 Douglas Avenue and is open from 10:00 A.M. to 5:00 P.M. Monday through Saturday and 1:00 P.M. to 5:00 P.M. on Sunday. Admission is $2 for adults and $1 for children two through eighteen and senior citizens. All Virginia students are free; (703) 632–1930.

Isle of Wight County

William A. Cheever's 1941 painting *Captain John Smith Trading with the Indians* is the WPA mural on the Smithfield Post Office wall at 234 West Main Street. It's said to be a scene from life at Burwell's Bay, 6 miles north on Route 10 out of Smithfield off Route 621.

Smithfield may be the "Ham Capital of the World," but that doesn't mean you can tour the Smithfield or Gwaltney (P. D. Gwaltney, Sr., started his curing process in 1870) ham processing plants. You can, however, smell the delicious aroma for miles around. The Smithfield process is protected by law, and only a ham cured within the Smithfield town limits can bear the name. You can visit some of the historic buildings in the area, and you won't be able to avoid seeing a lot of people driving to and from work. When the toll was taken off the James River Bridge, people moved south of the river and now commute to Newport News, Hampton, and other areas nearby.

The scenic Smithfield Old Town Walking Tour takes you past buildings dating from the mid- and late-1750s (the Old Courthouse and Clerk's Office at 130 Main Street and Pollard House at 108 Cary, the Old Jail at 106 North Mason and the Eason-Whitley House at 220 South Church, and others) up to pre–Civil War times. You can also view the four identical Victorian houses on Main Street and the Gingerbread Cottage on Grace Street. You can spend at least ninety minutes on this walk and expand it to three hours. Guided tours of the area, at $5 a person, are available (804) 357–7131).

The Isle of Wight County Museum in Smithfield, at the corner of Main and Church streets, is free and open on Sunday from 1:30 P.M. to 6:00 P.M. and Wednesday from 1:00 P.M. to 5:00 P.M. and by appointment (804) 357–7459).

Stop by the Chamber of Commerce and talk to Constance H. Rhodes. If you check at the Isle of Wight County Museum, R & R Limited gift shop, and other shops, you may find a series of ten postcards of scenes around the city by Smithfield native John B. Wynne. They cost $.50 each. Both of the shops above are on Main Street.

About two miles south of Smithfield on Route 10 is historic **St. Luke's Church,** known also as "Old Brick," the nation's only original Gothic church. Starting with the entrance, you'll find a wicket door within a larger door. Inside are a mid-seventeenth–century communion table and chairs, a seventeenth-century silver baptismal basin, original Gothic tracery windows, and a 1665 English organ. The church is open daily from 9:30 A.M. to 5:00 P.M., except Monday; it's closed all of January; (804) 357–3367.

Mecklenburg County

The 50,000-acre **Buggs Island Lake** straddling the North Carolina-Virginia border was constructed by the U.S. Army Corps of Engineers between 1946 and 1953 as one of a series of dams along the Roanoke River. It's really the John H. Kerr Dam and Reservoir (named after a North Carolina congressman who supported its construction), and the 169-acre Buggs Island is downstream of the dam. You can't tour the powerhouse, but you are welcome in the lobby, where you can see the generator and control room, or you can go to the Kerr Ridge Coffee Shoppe and Overlook. Besides 800 miles of shoreline with the expected water fun of fishing (striped bass or rockfish, crappie, and largemouth black bass, as well as hybrid muskie, bream, sunfish, carp, and garr), boating, and swimming, there are plenty of campgrounds and picnic and hunting areas. The activity that seems to be drawing the most attention here is the July Pontoon Boat Parade. Decorated like parade floats, the boats look like anything from pirate ships to trains.

Be sure to stop by the Bracey Welcome Station on Interstate 85 (if you're already in Virginia, you may have to go into North Carolina to do so) and say hello to Mildred Rhodes or Sandra Furr and their coworkers, for they are among the friendliest and most helpful people you'll ever meet. Call (804) 689–2892.

Nelson County

For thousands of people, a visit to **Schuyler** (pronounced *Skyler*) is mandatory once they reach Charlottesville, for it's the "real" home of Earl Hamner, the creator of *Walton's Mountain*. There is little resemblance between Schuyler and Walton, but as many as 500 people stop by every day (particularly on weekends) to visit "Ike's" general store, the Baptist Church, and the elemetary school and take a peek at the old homestead. Rosie Snead owns the country store, having purchased it about the same time the television series started, and during the summer she keeps it open seven days a week until 11:00 P.M. She must earn as much, or more, from selling postcards, the "real history" of the area, and color pictures of the Hammer house as she does from the rest of the merchandise in her store. Mrs. Hamner has not been well and visitors are requested not to disturb her. We have heard that someone, living in a house that looks considerably more like the one on the television show, will talk to visitors and will acknowledge that she is Mrs. Hamner (or Mrs. Walton, if you wish), but whether that's just a tale or is really happening we couldn't determine.

To reach Schuyler from Charlottesville, take Route 20 south to Route 6, near Scottsville. Turn right and follow Route 6 to Route 800. Turn left and go about 4 miles to Schuyler. To return, take Route 800 back to Route 6, but turn west and go north on Route 29.

Nottoway County

Originally, Blackstone was the village of the Blacks and Whites. This was so because of a rivalry between two tavern keepers, Schwartz (which is German for black) and White, rather than because of race relations. In 1885, the citizens adopted the name of noted English jurist Blackstone. It was the thirteenth town in the United States to adopt the town manager form of government. Nearby Camp Picket helped swell the town's population to 15,000 during World War II, and many retired military families have located here. Blackstone celebrated its centennial in 1988 by restoring some of the best turn-of-the-century storefronts and homes in Virginia. Awnings and period lampposts, representing Blackstone's Victorian heritage, edge the tree-lined street.

Armbruster's Restaurant in Blackstone offers the atmosphere of a restored 1908 home and traditional southern Virginia fare that includes Edwards country ham from Surry, chicken, seafood, beef, and seasonal offerings. Almost everything they make is from scratch, including three homemade dressings, corn pudding, and bread.

Armbruster's is operated by Bill and Betty Fraher Armbruster,

"Ike's"

who know their guests by their first names. A special periodic "spiritual guest" is Mrs. Robinson, who owned the residence and rented rooms until shortly before her death in 1967, and Bill says he thinks she still likes to entertain, and perhaps meet the "bootlegger," for Blackstone was dry in those days.

Betty is from Blackstone, and her parents lived in this home for some time following their marriage. Bill was in the Navy and always wanted to open a restaurant, which he did when he retired in October 1984. He says his major claim to food service experience was a job he held as a waiter in Williamsburg in one of the taverns while working his way through college.

On one of the walls is a picture of the Reserve Officers Training Camp in Fort Myer, May 1917, and you might want to see if you recognize anyone. Upstairs is a private dining room and a sitting area for wine and cheese prior to dinner. Some of the furniture is old family, some of it is from the house next door (where the doll museum is, see below), and some just came from flea markets and antique stores.

Armbruster's is open Tuesday through Saturday from 11:30 A.M. to 2:00 P.M. and 5:30 P.M. to 9:00 P.M. and Sunday from 11:30 A.M. to 4:00 P.M. It's at 205 Church Street; (804) 292–5992.

Next door is the Dollhouse Museum, a nonprofit operation housing an estimated 4,000 antique and modern dolls, dollhouses, toys, furniture, dishes, period clothing, and Americana. The collection is the result of a forty-year effort by Margaret Mills Armbruster (Bill Armbruster's mother). The most valuable doll is a French mechanical doll (still works) dating back to mid-1830s or 1840s. There's a perfectly huge and marvelous late-1800s display piece from a hardware store that closed in 1984. Upstairs is a model of the Trinity Lutheran Church in New London, Minnesota, where Arthur Ihlang (who built the model) was confirmed in 1906. It's complete with stained glass windows and a wedding in progress.

The museum first opened in New Port Richey, Florida, in 1972 and was known as Millie's Doll Museum. When her son and daughter-in-law opened Armbruster's Restaurant in Blackstone, she came north with her dolls. It took four rental trucks to bring everything to this marvelously refurbished two-story, eight-room Victorian home at 201 Church Street. It's open daily except Monday from 10:00 A.M. to noon and 1:00 P.M. to 4:00 P.M. and weekends from 2:00 P.M. to 5:00 P.M. Admission is $1.50 for adults and

50¢ for children. For special showings or information, call (804) 292–4007 or (804) 292–3487, or stop by the restaurant.

Patrick County

Two of the seven covered bridges remaining in Virginia are found in Patrick County, named for Patrick Henry. The Bob White Bridge is an 80-foot Theodore Burr bridge over the Smith River near Virginia Route 8, south of Woolwine. It was constructed in 1921 and served as the main link between Route 8 and a church on the south side of the river. It was used for more than a half-century before it was replaced by a newer bridge, but you still can walk up to the bridge, which has been kept as a landmark. Drive south from Woolwine on Route 8, about 1.5 miles, and then east 1 mile on Route 618 to Route 869, then south one-tenth of a mile.

Although it is called Jack's Creek Bridge, this covered bridge is over the Smith River on Route 615, just west of Virginia Route 8, about 2 miles south of Woolwine. You can see this 48-foot span from Route 8 where it intersects with Route 615, or travel about two-tenths of a mile west on Route 615.

Pittsylvania County

The largest county in the state is Pittsylvania County, where eighteenth-century houses still stand (pick up a map at the visitor center on 614 Lynn Street in Danville to visit them) and where there were more than thirty water mills with four—Tomahawk, Mt. Airy, Cedar Forest, and Stoney Mill—still in operation. History seems to be alive in this area, and if your group gives them enough notice, members of the Historical Society will dress in colonial costumes and entertain your busload at lunch. Genealogy can take on a new dimension in this county, for the courthouse records date from 1747, and the library has in-depth Virginia records and research tools. For Pittsylvania tours and information, call (804) 432–1669.

It's impossible to separate Danville from tobacco and textiles. Around the turn of the century there were between 90 and 100 tobacco companies, although only a few major ones remain.

Danville calls itself the "world's best tobacco market" and is the home of the world's largest single-unit textile mill. It's also the place where, on September 27, 1903, a southbound mail express train on the Southern Railroad left the tracks on a trestle and plunged into the ravine below, where nine people were killed. This incident was the inspiration for the song "The Wreck of the Old '97" and is recorded on a historical marker on Highway 58 between Locust Lane and North Main Street.

In place of all the fall foliage festivals held along the Shenandoah Valley, the agricultural areas of Virginia's central-southside enjoy harvest festivals and fairs. Danville is home to the annual World Tobacco Auctioneering Championship, part of the fall Danville Harvest Jubilee, held about the second weekend in October. Join the estimated 40,000 people attending this multi-day offering of music, a 5-K run, a home and garden show, belly bucking (which is just what is sounds like—two rotund bellies battling each other), fireworks, an all-you-can-eat shrimp fest, a rabbit breeders show, a clogging competition and the Harvest Ball in Piedmont Mall.

In tobacco jargon, flue-curing is a heat-curing process producing a bright, golden-colored tobacco that dries more quickly than air-cured tobacco from farther north. Regular auctions of flue-cured tobacco, which began in 1858, are held Monday through Thursday from mid-August through early November at ten auction offices, making Danville Virginia's largest loose-leaf tobacco auction center.

Before you attend an auction or the championship, stop by the **Tobacco and Textile Museum** to view the fifteen-minute tape about auctioneering and the ten-minute film about tobacco so you'll understand what's happening. One half of the museum is dedicated to the tobacco crop and displays sculptures made of tobacco leaves, pipes, and old and current cigarette packages. Of particular interest is the "Lucky Strike Goes to War" exhibit showing the change in package color. In 1942, because the war effort needed the copper powder and chromium used in printing the gold and green colors of the package, Lucky Strike packages became red and gray on a white background. It's said enough copper was saved in a year to buy bronze for 400 light military tanks. You'll also learn that tobacco is a labor intensive crop that takes about 400 hours per acre to grow and harvest, while other crops take as little as 1 to 4 hours per acre.

On the other side of the museum is an exhibit of the textile industry that illustrates how cotton becomes material and includes a model with 8,000 intricately carved, turned, and jig-sawed pieces of a Dan River finishing plant made by Gary Johnson for a display in the Smithsonian Institution in Washington, D.C. It shows some of the fifty-two steps usually involved in processing and finishing the cotton material. Mr. Dempsey Deehart and Mr. Sam Scott helped assemble the model under the supervision of a Mr. Schollenberger. His wife, Grace Schollenberger, fashioned the models representing employees at work. The model was returned from the Smithsonian and donated to the Danville museum in 1974.

The museum is not fancy marble and high-tech lighting but is appropriate for its location— in a former tobacco processing plant. The Tobacco and Textile Museum is also the Danville Visitor Center and there's usually someone at the information counter by 8:30 A.M. The information people will tell you about tours of the tobacco warehouses and auctions. There's also a gift shop at the museum and displays of an old marble soda fountain and original ads for PepsiCola, with copies for sale at the gift shop.

Museum hours are from 10:00 A.M. to 4:00 P.M. Admission is $1.50 for adults and 75¢ for children. The museum is located at 614 Lynn Street in the warehouse district; (804) 797–9437.

As you drive through Danville, you near the North Carolina line, and by the time you pass the Green Tree Restaurant and Motel, you're into the Tarheel State. Do take some time to drive or walk through Millionaire's Row, eight blocks of one of the finest collections of Victorian and Edwardian architecture in the South. Start at 975 Main Street, at the restored antebellum Sutherlin house, known as the Last Capitol of the Confederate States of America. Jefferson Davis signed his last official resolution here before the Confederacy fell on April 9, 1865. This 1857 Italianate villa-style house is now the Danville Museum of Fine Arts and History.

Tours are available Tuesday through Friday, 10:00 A.M. to 5:00 P.M. and Sunday 2:00 P.M. to 5:00 P.M. You can take a short tour down to 871 Main Street or a longer tour down to Sutherlin Avenue to a 1900 Romanesque Revival edifice that is now the home of Temple Beth Sholom. Pick up a Victorian Walking Tour brochure at the visitor center. The homes are closed most of the year, but are open the second Sunday in December for the Danville Historical Society's annual Christmas Walking Tour.

Chatham has won several Keep Virginia Beautiful awards and has earned a reputation as the prettiest little town in the southside. The **Pittsylvania County Museum** has aritfacts from Revolutionary and Civil War days, with a series of five dioramas depicting Gen. Nathanael Greene's immortal race to the Dan, which took place about 35 miles from Chatham. The Chatham Post Office at Main and Pitt streets has another of the two dozen WPA murals, this one by Danville artist Carson Davenport. Completed in 1938, the agricultural mural *Harvest Season in Southern Virginia* has Davenport's name on the tobacco packing crate on the right edge of the painting.

The Pittsylvania County Schools' Planetarium is in Chatham with fairly regular shows, and if weather permits, at least one of the planetarium's telescopes (two are 8-inch reflectors and one is a $17\frac{1}{2}$-inch reflector) is open for programs.

Williamsburg is not the only place to benefit from the donations of DeWitt Wallace (*Reader's Digest*), for he also helped fund the restoration of the Yates Tavern in Gretna. Dating back to about 1750, the basement has rock walls about 2 feet thick. The 10-inch front and back overhangs, known as jetties, provide additional upper living space and make the Yates Tavern the only such old dwelling in Virginia. In restoration, original eighteenth-century materials, such as a collapsing structure from Laurel Grove, an old cabin from Red Oak Hollow, and an old Danville structure, were used rather than reproductions. Yates is open on Sunday from 2:00 P.M. to 5:00 P.M., May through October; (804) 432-1669.

Prince Edward County

A handsome new granite and bronze **monument,** dedicated to the Reverend **Francis E. Griffin,** stands on the grounds of the Farmville Elementary School, formerly the Robert R. Moton High School. It faces Griffin Boulevard, formerly Eli Street, in Farmville. The Town Council renamed the street after the 1980 death of Griffin, former minister of the First Baptist Church. Known as a man who "knew that democracy was not a spectator sport," he became a participant in the civil rights issues of the 1950s. Called "the fighting preacher" and the "love preacher," his aid was sought when the high school went on strike in 1951 to protest the lack of equal facilities when compared to the "white" school. The court suit that followed was one of five heard by the United States Supreme Court that challenged the separate-but-equal doctrine.

Prince George County

Even though Petersburg is nicely promoted and has many different types of attractions, there are a few things that are still off the beaten path.

There are two WPA murals in Petersburg, both in the post office at 29 Franklin Street. One, *Riding to Hounds,* by Edwin S. Lewis, is about fox hunting (he did the mural in the Berryville Post Office), and supposedly his wife is portrayed as the central figure in this painting. The second, on the east wall, is by William Calfee (who did the Tazewell and Phoebus murals as well), a more pastoral scene entitled *Agriculture Scenes in Virginia* with tobacco on one side and peanuts on the other. Also in the post office, in one of the display boxes, is a history of the Petersburg postal service dating back to 1773 that includes a list of all eighteen postmasters who served (some served multiple terms) in this Petersburg office up to the present.

Neighborhood tours are given every Sunday at 2:00 P.M. (except winter months) featuring one of twenty or thirty different neighborhoods, with a tour of the Blandford Cemetery about once a month. Write to Historic Petersburg, P.O. Box 2107, Petersburg 23804, or call for the schedule (804–733–2402).

Of the items on the Petersburg tour, two seem to be more outstanding than others. The first is **Blandford Church and Cemetery** on 321 South Crater Road, the highest spot in the Petersburg area. Start your tour of the church and cemetery at the interpretation center with a free eighteen-minute slide show that starts about every thirty minutes.

Not only is the church, with its inverse ship's hull ceiling design, a Confederate memorial, it's one of the art treasures of the country. It's known for its fifteen magnificent Louis Comfort Tiffany stained glass windows. The church was built in 1735, and they say it's the only building in the country with every window an original Tiffany production. The original plan called for windows to represent each of the Confederate states, each depicting one of the Apostles, and smaller ones for the states whose sympathies had been divided. The windows took eight years to complete, and each cost between $100 (for the smaller Maryland window) and $400, including shipping. The Cross of Jewels window was donated by Tiffany.

If possible, you might want to see the church twice or even three times: the first when there isn't much sun, the second when there's a brilliant sun, and the third at sunset, to see the magnificent beauty of the Cross of Jewels. The work really is gorgeous and some of the detail beyond description and belief. The windows change almost moment by moment with a three-dimensional effect coming from the Tiffany talents. Three visits may seem a large demand on your time, but these windows are worth it. The church was restored in 1901 through the efforts of the Ladies Memorial Association of Petersburg, whose remembrances of the war dead started our Memorial Day tradition.

The donation for touring the church is $2 for adults and $1 for seniors and children. Residents of Petersburg are admitted free. Services are held here about once a month, and the newspapers are supposed to carry notice of the exact dates and times. Blandford Church Memorial Day services are held on June 9 each year; (804) 733-2396.

The cemetery began before the church building was constructed, and the oldest known grave dates to 1702. Some of the finest examples of cast and wrought iron in the nation are found here. Many locals are buried here, along with 30,000 Confederate soldiers who were brought in from other areas. British Gen. Williams Phillips was buried here, secretly—the only British general to have been buried in American soil for many, many years.

Over in Old Towne Petersburg (which was referred to as Old Towne two hundred years ago) is the Petersburg tour's second most outstanding attraction, the **Siege Museum,** which tells the tale of life in Petersburg during the ten months of 1889 when the city was under attack, the longest of any city during the Civil War. Conditions were terrible, and the museum shows the war's effect on the economy, industry, and the people themselves. Start with the film, shown every hour on the hour, and then wander through to learn how to the women were the real heroes. You'll see two bullets that met midair and fused. Also on display is one of the only two revolving cannons ever built—the first exploded when it was fired and the second was never fired. View the photos, eye-witness descriptions, and artifacts. Learn how ladies' hoop skirts hid food, supplies, and ammunition for the defenders. The museum is in the former Bank of Petersburg and it, like the other 800 buildings in the city, was under attack for two to three hours a day.

The U.S. Army Quartermaster Corps is the branch of the service that supplies food, clothing, and military equipment to our armed forces. The U.S. Army Quartermaster Museum at Fort Lee (formerly Camp Lee) shows life-size exhibits of colorful uniforms, weapons, Pershing's office furniture, General Patton's jeep, and furniture from Eisenhower and Kennedy's offices. You'll also see a drum used in President Kennedy's funeral cortege and the architect's original model for the Tomb of the Unknown Soldier. There is no admission charge, and the museum is open daily from 8:00 A.M. to 5:00 P.M. and on Saturday, Sunday, and holidays from 11:00 A.M. to 5:00 P.M., but it's closed on Thanksgiving, Christmas, and New Year's. Take Route 36 east from Petersburg and the museum is just inside the main gate on A Avenue. Call (804) 734-1854 for more information.

Not too far from Petersburg is the Hopewell and City Point Historic District, where you can view the confluence of the Appomattox and James rivers. This small, bustling town adjacent to Fort Lee had a population of 40,000 during World War I, with an additional 65,000 at the then Camp Lee. The DuPont Nemours plant was known for making guncotton for dynamite. At the end of the war, Hopewell's population returned to 1,369, about the same as after the Civil War. Local historian Mary M. Calos has prepared a walking and driving tour description unlike most others. Mrs. Calos can tell you about Revolutionary War history, the famous pecan tree, and the misplaced historical marker for Fort Abbott. Write 201 D Randolph Square, Hopewell 23860 or call (804) 541-2206.

If you've been tracing the trail of the WPA murals and sculptures through the two dozen post office buildings in Virginia, you've noticed a similarity in style and execution even though the paintings were created by many different artists. Now look at Edmund Archer's painting, *Captain Francis Eppes Making Friends with the Appomattox Indians,* at the Hopewell Post Office at 117 West Pythress Street. The gesture of friendship is melodramatic and physically impossible—try to imitate the postures of the two men and see if you can keep your balance. Perhaps you should not do this in the post office, though. Mrs. Calos says Captain Eppes arrived in 1635 with a land grant of about 1,700 acres. He came on the ship *Hopewell,* which gave the city its name.

A little farther east (off Route 10 and then 639) is **Flowerdew Hundred,** where the cultural history of the plantation and its region is studied and interpreted. The area surrounding Flowerdew was one of the earliest English settlements and was inhabited by American Indians before that. More than sixty-five sites have been explored through archaeological digs since 1971, and thousands of items, some dating from 9000 B.C., have been uncovered and many are on display in the museum. The eighteenth-century–style windmill has been reconstructed and is operational. Reproductions, cornmeal ground at the windmill, and other items are for sale at the museum shop and bookstore. Flowerdew Hundred is open April 1 through November 30 from 10:00 A.M. to 5:00 P.M. Admission is $2.50 for adults, $1.50 for children 6–12, and free for those under 6. Call (804) 541-8897.

Richmond

For pure architectural and historical enjoyment of a nonorganized nature, visit Richmond's Fan District, bordered by Monroe Park, the Boulevard, and Monument Avenue on the north and Cary Street on the south. A suburb of this bustling town back in the 1890s, the Fan District is now incorporated into the city of Richmond. At one time the height of fashion, then nearly abandoned, it's once more "the" place to be. The mile-square, tree-lined district of streets radiate or fan out, and a map slightly resembles the fashionable accessory southern ladies are so noted for—and surely, as modern as Richmond has become, she is still a southern lady. The town houses carry traces of Victorian, Greek Revival, Italianate, Tudor, or Georgian touches. They're joined by party walls or separated by narrow walkways.

A visit and tour of the 1790 **Capitol** is a special treat, particularly the hidden dome Jefferson designed in the Italian-architecture–inspired building. Free tours are given by docents from 9:00 A.M. to 5:00 P.M., with the last full tour starting at 4:30 P.M., seven days a week (1:00 P.M. to 5:00 P.M. on Sundays from

November to March). You'll also receive a free booklet about the Capitol. The large equestrian statue of George Washington in the northwest corner of the square was constructed to be his final resting place, before his body was buried at Mount Vernon. If you're interested and can find an agreeable guard, you can climb up the inside of the statue. The Capitol is at Ninth and Grace streets; (804) 786-4334.

A $50 million world-class botanical garden is set for the north end of Richmond at Bloemendaal, a beautiful home located on a small pond. The **Lewis Ginter Botanical Garden** should include three domed greenhouse pavilions, seven major gardens, a four-acre lake, a 250-seat auditorium, restaurant, three fountains, an arboretum, and a horticultural school. The design was prepared by Geoffrey Raush of Environmental Planning and Design in Pittsburgh, a firm that has served as consultant to botanical gardens in Chicago and St. Louis. Some of the gardens, the home, and the visitor center are open now, daily from 9:30 A.M. to 4:30 P.M., with some seasonal alteration. There is no admission charge, but a donation of $1.50 is requested. Call (804) 262-9887 for more details.

For walking or bus tours of the city that might include the theater district, Art Deco buildings, or other architectural or historical points, call (804) 780-0107. You bring your own brown bag lunch and the tour charge is $1.

A superb overlook of the city is off of East Broad Street, west up 23rd Street, with a right turn on Grace Street until it deadends, where you can view downtown Richmond. It is particularly beautiful on a clear night.

Taking a tour through the **Philip Morris manufacturing plant** south of downtown Richmond is like going through a miniride at a theme park, for you're placed on a tram to witness the world's largest and most modern cigarette facility. There's a small museum of tobacco-related artifacts (not nearly the scope of the one in Danville), and then you visit the area where 500 to 550 million cigarettes are rolled each day. This is high-tech business. Take the Bells Road exit off Interstate 95 and follow the signs; (804) 274-3342.

For scientific technology of another sort, you should visit the **Science Museum of Virginia,** otherwise just called the Universe. Actually, the Universe is "the planetarium and cinema of the future," for the museum has a 280-seat auditorium with a hemispheric 76-foot diameter screen that envelops you totally with its protections. The facility has the world's first computer graphics projector, Digistar 1, along with over a hundred special effects projectors and 108-speaker sound system.

This is definitely a hands-on museum, and you're invited to discover and explore the scientific world in language and displays that reach all levels. Other attractions at the museum are the computer works sections, where you can pick up the basics or go one-on-one against the superbrains. After you've played mind games, head for the visual perception area and play games with your eyesight with mirrors and other optical illusions. Five crystal-shaped structures fill the rotunda floor, and those crystals house a complete display on the formation of crystals and their importance.

The science museum is located in the former Broad Street Railroad Station. Originally opened in 1919, the building was designed by John Russell Pope. Hours are 10:00 A.M. to 5:00 P.M. Monday through Saturday and 11:00 A.M. to 5:00 P.M. on Sunday. The shows at the Universe run on their own schedule. A combination ticket costs $3.00 to $3.50, and a museum-only ticket costs $1.00 to $1.50. The Universe is at 2500 West Broad Street, (804) 367–1013; for information about the planetarium call (804) 25–STARS.

Assuming you've noted the brightly colored and decorative flags hanging from Sixth Street Marketplace and the Science Museum (and almost anyplace you see a flag or banner), you'll want to visit Millie Jones at Festival Flags, 322 West Broad Street. Millie accidently started this "cottage" industry in the mid-1970s when she created a flag to identify her new home in the Fan for party guests. Other flags followed, including one announcing "It's a boy" when her son Jonathan arrived. Friends started ordering flags, and soon a sewing machine in the house wasn't sufficient. Now she's located in new quarters and has a dozen seamstresses (the number keeps growing) and artists working for her, and her flags have flown on the *Godspeed* and in a space shuttle and just about any other place you can imagine. You can buy one off the rack (flagpole) or give her or Diana Hough a design you want her to execute or tell her what you want and let her create it for you. Prices generally range from about $35 to $350. The one-of-a-kind, three-dimensional butterfly in the showroom is gorgeous, but Millie doesn't seem too anxious for anyone to buy it. No one can blame her. Call (804) 643–5247.

Lyn Benson is a dynamo of activity who has brought several bed-and-breakfast home owners together into an organization called **Bensonhouse of Richmond.** Her forty homes may be along Monument Avenue or out in the country, and her guests are people on wedding trips or anniversaries, business people who don't want to spend long stays in a hotel, and normal people who want to take time to know people in Richmond. Write 2036 Monument Avenue, Richmond 23220 or call (804) 648–7560.

According to Charles Ingram, post office maintenance supervisor, the two sets of WPA murals in Richmond have been removed and placed in storage, although he's not sure where they are or what's to become of them. In any case, two artists were involved in producing the paintings for the old Richmond Parcel Post Building (now part of the Federal Center at 1100 East Main Street, but the building does carry the old Parcel Post legend). One set of panels, measuring 20 feet by $7^1/_2$ feet, was by Jared French, interpreting *Stuart's Raiders at the Swollen Ford.* The other was by Paul Cadmus, entitled *Dawn, April 3, 1865.* Both were done in 1939.

Planted firmly in mid-tap at Leigh and Adams streets is the statue of Bill "Bojangles" Robinson, noted tap dancer and entertainer, by Ashland sculptor Jack Witt. Robinson was born at 915 North Third Street in Richmond's Jackson Ward neighborhood. He gave money for a traffic signal at this corner to help the neighborhood children safely cross the street and to a variety of other charitable causes, and in 1973 the City of Richmond erected this statue in his honor. He's portrayed as we all remember him, tap dancing down (or up) a flight of stairs. (Witt has another life-size sculpture, a bronze of a street jester, in front of the Grace Street entrance to the Sixth Street Marketplace.)

The Carillon, located in Byrd Park, is a 240-foot Georgian bell tower (466 feet above sea level) dedicated to the memory of those who served in World War I. It's recently undergone a $1,400,000 renovation, and recitals of the fifty-six bells (orginally sixty-six bells covering four and half octaves) are scheduled for Sunday afternoon at 4:00 P.M. during the spring and early summer months. The bell deck is reached by an elevator, and from there you can take steps to the observation platforms. The Singing Tower is made of brick and stone, with a large bronze door giving entrance to an octagonal room 30 feet in height. Gallery space is available for shows. The Carillon is near the entrance to the Dogwood Dell outdoor theater, just north of Boulevard Bridge; (804) 780–8136.

Two hundred years ago, the James River Company started the canals on the James River that would allow navigation around the 7 miles of fall line in and above Richmond. The Kanawha Canal Locks are part of the dream George Washington had of a waterway system from the Midwest to the Atlantic. The James River runs 125 miles (by water) to Hampton Roads, and there was 200 miles of river north of the city into the Alleghenies. From there it was only 33 miles to the Kanawha River and its tributaries, the New and Greenbrier, which flow west into the Ohio and on to the Mississippi. Two Kanawha Canal Locks built in 1854 for this first canal system constructed in North America have been preserved by the Reynolds Metals Company as part of the design of the Reynolds Wrap Distribution Center at 12th and Byrd streets. Each lock is 100 feet long by 15 feet wide and made of stone, but the lock gates, constructed of wood, rotted out in the last of the nineteenth century. You can visit the locks, go fishing, have a picnic, and view an audiovisual presentation of the canal's history.

Further south at Pear and Dock streets, you'll find the line where salt water from the Atlantic Ocean meets the fresh water from the James River. Picnic tables are available. Much work is planned for the north bank of the James River, with hopes that the urban recreation area someday will look, feel, and be like the San Antonio Riverwalk in Texas.

Noted for years as the most beautiful roadway in America, the 1.3 miles of Monument Avenue was paved by hand shortly after the turn of the century. It's framed with trees and marvelous old houses, and down its center spine are statues of Com. M. F. Maury, Jefferson Davis, Maj. Gen. J. E. B. Stuart, Gen. Thomas Jonathan "Stonewall" Jackson (both Stuart and Jackson were battlefield casualties and both monuments face north) and Robert E. Lee (facing south). It's said that military statues are supposed to be dressed in full military uniform and that it's not proper to be shown without your hat on; but the story goes that the sculptor thought Lee's brow was so proud that he could not cover it up.

The 1895 **Jefferson Hotel,** a massive, white brick hotel blending Louis XVI and Colonial Renaissance, was once the finest hostelry in the South. It burned in 1901 and again in 1944. Now, after the benefit of an estimated $40,000,000 renovation and restoration, it's been renamed the Jefferson Sheraton Hotel. The glorious colors of the magnificent stained glass dome once again radiate into the Palm Court lobby below. Live alligators lived in the two reflecting pools in the Palm Court lobby from the early 1900s until 1948, with "Old Poppy" being one of particular note. Several of the bellhops of that period have told stories of finding the alligators crawling on the upholstered chairs in the lobby and having to chase them back into their pools. The restoration finds the alligators enshrined in bronze, permanently situated at the foot of the Thomas Jefferson statue; however, when the Ringling Brothers, Barnum and Bailey Circus came to town, they brought a real alligator to the Jefferson for some publicity photos. You never know what you'll find here. Just be sure when you put your feet up on a foot stool that it doesn't walk away. The grand staircase, which legend says was the model for the staircase in *Gone With the Wind,* is back. Film buffs might recognize the hotel from the film *My Dinner with André,* which was shot at this location. The Jefferson's Grand Ballroom features the original chandelier and gold detailed ceiling. The hotel is at Franklin and Adams streets; (804) 788–8000.

For additional tourism information, write to the Metropolitan Richmond Convention and Visitors Bureau, 300 East Main Street, Richmond 23219, or call (804) 782–2777 or (800) 365–7272.

Sussex County

The first commercial peanut crop grown in Virginia was grown in Sussex County in 1844, and today peanuts represent a multi-million–dollar industry in the state, so it's not surprising that you'll find peanut this and peanut that all along Route 460 and throughout the southside. The peanut, filled with protein, is the basis for several cookbooklets, which include recipes for crunchy chicken bits, cookies, glazed peanut bread, peanut-stuffed squash, peanut party biscuits, wine cheese logs, cream of peanut soup, peanut broccoli salad, peanut spinach balls, oriental crepes, peachy peanut spread, and, of course, peanut butter pie. Write to Production Promotion, Division of Markets, Virginia Department of Agriculture and Consumer Services, P.O. Box 1163, Richmond 23209 for copies.

For miles along Route 460, before you come to Wakefield, you'll see billboards announcing how many miles it is to the **Virginia Diner,** noted for its treatment of peanuts. It's an old 125-seat diner that is singularly unimpressive in appearance, but don't let that deceive you. Bill Galloway has Virginia Fancy and Virginia Jumbos, which he first boils in water, then roasts in his special vegetable oil (he says the peanuts blister, giving them extra crunch). A one-pound bag is about $3.15 and is available from P.O. Box 310, Wakefield 23888. Call (804) 899–3106.

Across the street is Plantation Peanuts, with a select variety of nuts chosen for their classic style and flavor. Each batch is slightly cooked and hand salted (ask them how they salt peanuts in the shell), and it's all done in the back room, except for the candied or sugared nuts, which are prepared elsewhere. A two-pound bag of roasted peanuts in the shell or fancy roasted is $4.95 and is available from P.O. Box 610, Wakefield 23888; call (804) 899–8407.

Surry County

Bacon's Castle doesn't exactly look like a castle, but the 1665 high Jacobean-style structure is said to be the oldest known brick dwelling in North America, and it has given its name to the area. Built by Arthur Allen, it was seized and occupied for three months in 1676 by rebel troops supporting the rebel Nathaniel Bacon in an event known as Bacon's Rebellion. The building has Dutch-gabled ends and triple diamond stack chimneys on each end, and it has been purchased by the Association for the Preservation of Virginia Antiquities. Two rooms are furnished from the original inventory, and there are archaeological and architectural exhibits offered, as well as a slide show. One of the digs has uncovered an old trash pit with an "AA" (for Arthur Allen) bottle seal on it.

Guided tours are available from mid-April through September, noon to 4:00 P.M. Tuesday through Sunday and 10:00 A.M. to 4:00 P.M. on Saturday. Adults are $4 and children $1. It's open by appointment at other times. Bacon's Castle is just off the intersection of Route 10 and Route 31. For details, call (804) 359–0239 or (804) 229–9485.

The **Scotland-Jamestown Ferry,** or the Jamestown-Scotland Ferry, clearance 12 feet, 6 inches, connects Route 31 over the James River and leaves just about every half hour from a little after 5:00 A.M. until midnight, with longer hours and more frequent trips during the summer. The tolls range from $1 for two-axle vehicles to $6 for multi-axle, mutli-unit vehicles; for pedestrians or bicycles, the toll is $.15.

Index

Index

Index

Index

Index

About the Authors

Judy and Ed Colbert have spent years traveling and camping in Virginia and have family and friends throughout the state. They live in the neighboring state of Maryland where Ed works full-time as a television production manager with the U.S. Government and Judy conducts a prolific writing career.

An award-winning free-lance writer and photographer, she covers travel primarily, and her articles and photographs have appeared in such publications as *Washingtonian, McCall's, Washington Post, Mid-Atlantic Country, Dallas Morning News, USA Today,* and *Spa Vacations.*

She is coauthor with her husband of *The Spa Guide,* published by The Globe Pequot Press, and Judy has appeared as an expert in travel and spas on numerous radio and television shows, including "Good Morning America" and Arthur Frommer's "Almanac of Travel" show.

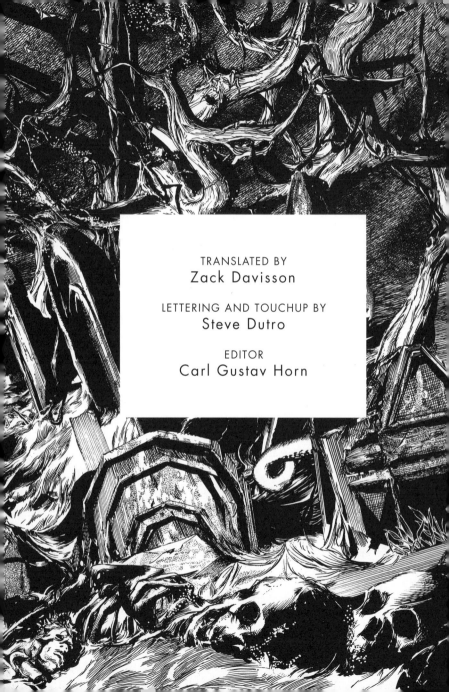

TRANSLATED BY
Zack Davisson

LETTERING AND TOUCHUP BY
Steve Dutro

EDITOR
Carl Gustav Horn

All of these graphic novellas are
based on stories by
Howard Phillips "H. P." Lovecraft

contents

神　殿

THE TEMPLE

H. P. LOVECRAFT'S
"THE TEMPLE"
Written in 1920
Published in September 1925 in *Weird Tales*

On the afternoon of June 18, we torpedoed the British freighter Victory at N. Latitude 45° 16', W. Longitude 28° 34'.

I am Karl Heinrich, Graf von Altberg-Ehrenstein, in command of the U-29.

9

HMM...

...FROM HEAD-QUARTERS.

SIR...

FWAP!!

OUR BOAT...

...SHALL INTERCEPT THE BRITISH LINER *DACIA*.

...OUR RETURN TO WILHELMS-HAVEN IS POST-PONED.

...

SHIP AHOY.

AYE, SIR!

DUMP IT OVERBOARD.

CREW O' THAT BRITISH FREIGHTER, WE RECKON!

SIR!

DEAD BODY ON DECK...FROM YESTERDAY...

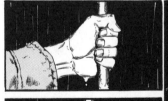

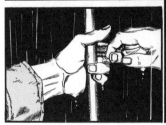

TOMMY'S STIFF BY NOW.

QUITE A GRIP FOR A DEAD MAN...

WELL, PRY HIM OFF.

FWUMP

NOW...

...GRAB THE FEET.

HM...

NOW WHAT'S THIS...?

HO!

LT. KLENZE...?

YOU.

WAIT.

?

RUSTLE

RUSTLE

14

RIGHT. PITCH HIM OVER.

?

...'EY!!

SPLASHHH

MÜLLER'S GONE SENILE...

FOOL!

HE SWAM AWAY...!

!

...YOU SEE?!

LOOK, BOHM...

HE'S DEAD. A WAVE CARRIED HIM OFF...

NO...

...I SAW WHAT I SAW.

SIR, SOME OF THE CREW, THEY'RE...

YES?

SICK...

RETURN...

THE DEAD... THE DEAD...

HOLD FAST, BOHM...

THAT TOMMY...

NERVOUS EXHAUS- TION.

TAKE THEM OFF DUTY.

...DEAD!

...

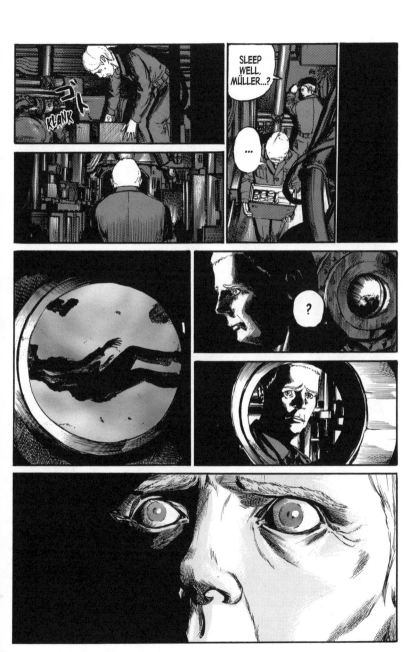

HE... H...

...!

AAAAAA!!

OUT THE PORT-HOLE...

MÜLLER! WHAT IS IT NOW...?

YOU MUST GIVE IT BACK...

LIEU-TENANT!

I SAW HIM AGAIN...

THE BRITISHER...?

KLENZE.

...THE PATH OF THE DEAD...

HE TAKES...

...OLD FOOL?

SMACK

TO A CORPSE...

20

UP, YOU!

TAKE HIM TO THE BRIG.

AYE, SIR?

HE IS THEIR LORD...

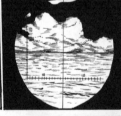

ゴコゴコ
RMM RMM RMM

EH?

COM-MANDER...

MÜLLER AND BOHM ARE BOTH MISSING...

THEY MUST HAVE JUMPED OFF WHEN WE LAST SURFACED. DID ANYONE SEE...?

NO.

...

WELL, THEN. COLLECT THEIR BELONGINGS.

AYE, SIR.

22

NO, SIR.

ANY WORD FROM HQ?

THE *DACIA* ELUDED US...

AS THERE ARE NO ORDERS, WE SHALL RETURN TO WILHELMS-HAVEN.

SEND TO HQ...

I'M GOING TO KISS THE FIRST DIRT I SEE...!

AYE, SIR!!

40 DAYS ON PATROL...!

NO CONTACT WITH *DACIA*.

HEAD-ING FOR BASE.

SET COURSE.

23

THE ENGINE ROOM...!

SIR!!

AN EXPLOSION ...?

FWSSSHHHH
ゴ ゴ ゴ

DAMAGE REPORT...?

STEERING COLUMN'S A WRECK AS WELL.

...FUEL'S GONE.

ENGINE CREW KILLED...

ON BATTERY POWER.

AYE, SIR.

CAN WE STILL SURFACE?

WE'RE DEAD IN THE WATER, SIR.

...

LET'S AT LEAST SEE WHERE WE ARE.

グブブ
RRRRMMMM

On July 2 we made enemy contact.

27

TRAUBE, TO STATIONS.

SIR, LET'S SURRENDER.

WILL YOU OBEY?

...WHEN THE AIR AND POWER GIVE OUT, WE'LL JUST SINK INTO THE ABYSS...

SIR, WHAT'S THE POINT? WE CAN'T MANEUVER ...

BLAMMM

SIR, IT'S OVER. OPEN THE HATCH...

WE'VE GOT TO...

28

...

ALL HANDS TO STATIONS.

THUD

GET HIM OFF THE BRIDGE.

HM?

LIEU-TENANT ...

GIVE IT BACK, SIR. GIVE IT BACK TO THE SEA.

WILL YOU OBEY...?

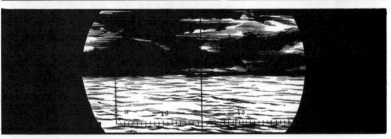

ゴゥ ゴゥ
GGRRRRNNNNN

NOTHING, SIR.

ANY SOUND OF THE SHIP?

WE ESCAPED THE ENEMY.

The mutiny occurred at 5 AM on July 4.

BAMMM

...?

SPKKK FZZR

WELL ...?

...SHAME-LESS.

ALL OF YOU...

THEY'RE ANGRY WE DIDN'T SURRENDER TO THAT YANKEE SHIP.

I BEG YOU...MAYBE SOMEONE WILL STILL RESCUE US...

SIR... RAISE SHIP!

SAILORS OF THE FATHERLAND DO NOT SURRENDER.

YOU'VE FORGOTTEN YOUR GERMAN PRIDE.

...TO THE ABYSS...THE BLACK ABYSS...

THE TOMMY IS LEADING US...

N... NO!

FOR GOD'S SAKE, SIR...

ゴゴゴ
RRRRMMMM

KLAK
カ!カ

KLENZE, WE CANNOT RETURN.

WHILE FOOD AND AIR REMAIN...

..WE MUST CONSIDER HOW TO FULFILL OUR DUTY.

WITH THE CREW DEAD, THERE'S FOOD AND AIR ENOUGH.

BUT THE BATTERIES WILL GO FIRST.

GULG ヒ゛ ヒ゛ GULG

US TWO?

YES.

...

WE'LL BE IN THE DARK...

Our instruments were destroyed during the mutiny. Our only method of estimating speed, and hence approximate position, is by observing our rate of movement through the portholes.

The unexplained explosion has rendered propulsion impossible. Six days have passed... we continue to drift.

I'LL NEED MORE DATA...

ANY GOOD...?

THE SUNKEN SHIP...?

SIR, LOOK.

...

JUST A CLIFF, KLENZE.

IT'S...

NO...NEXT TO IT...

IT'S SCULPTED...

...THAT SEA CLIFF...

LIEU-TENANT...

SIR... I...

...IT MUST BE MY NERVES.

...EXCUSE ME, SIR...

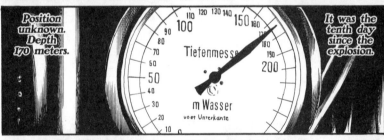

Position unknown. Depth 170 meters.

It was the tenth day since the explosion.

GOD...

...SAVE ME.

37

GOD.

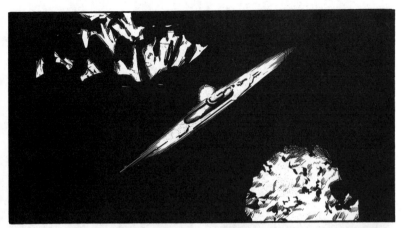

HE
CALLS...

LET'S GO...

...BEST TO REPENT AND BE FORGIVEN.

REFUSE. IT CHANGES NOTHING...

WE GO TOGETHER.

THAT IS MERCY.

YOU'RE INSANE.

PITY THE MAN WHOSE CALLOUS-NESS...

SO...

BEG FOR HIS MERCY... GO MAD.

...KEEPS HIM SANE.

SIR...

...

HEH HEH HEH...

IF YOU WON'T GO...

...ALLOW ME TO.

LEAVE THE ARTIFACT.

44

...YOU ARE TOO SANE.

ANY MESSAGE FOR YOUR FAMILY?

HEH... I SEE THAT...

...WHEN I CLOSE THE INTERNAL HATCH, PULL THE LEVER.

I...

KLENZE. WAIT.

45

CHAKK

KLANGG

WHSHHHHHHHH

46

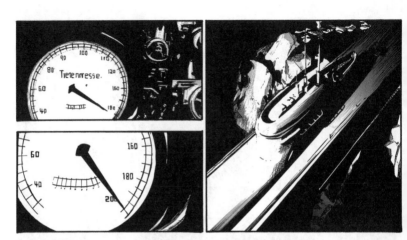

I looked for Klenze's body...

...and the deep.

...but there were only dolphins...

Perhaps there is yet hope.

Observations suggest the speed of drift has slowed. It is difficult to determine my current position.

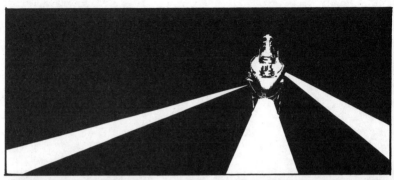

..is falling away steeply.

The forward seabed...

...a strange formation.

Adjusting the searchlight...

...I perceived...

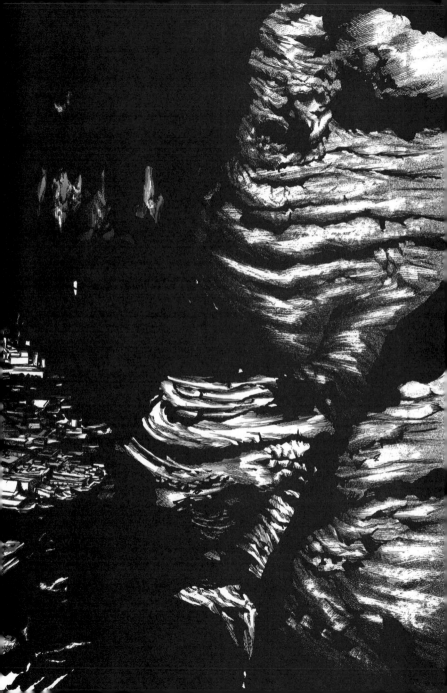

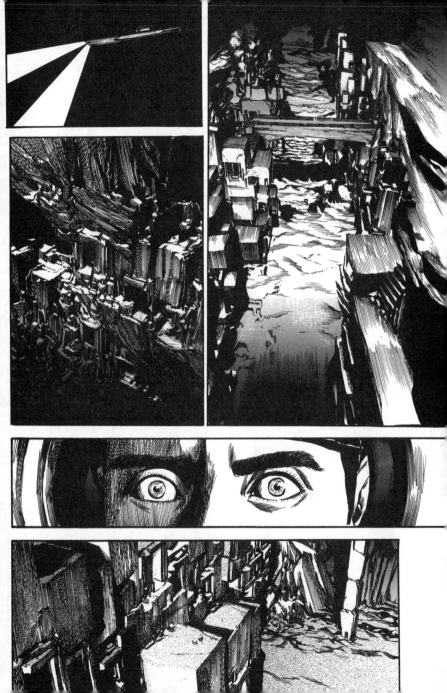

...yet a civilization rested on the ocean floor.

So deep...

I had deemed it a myth...but before my eyes was the legendary city.

Atlantis!

...to tread these aeon-forgotten ways!

...shall be the first...

I, a Reichsdeutscher...

It was not built, but carved, in every detail, from the virgin hillside rock of our planet. It is palpably a part of the sea valley wall.

I could scarcely believe what I perceived.

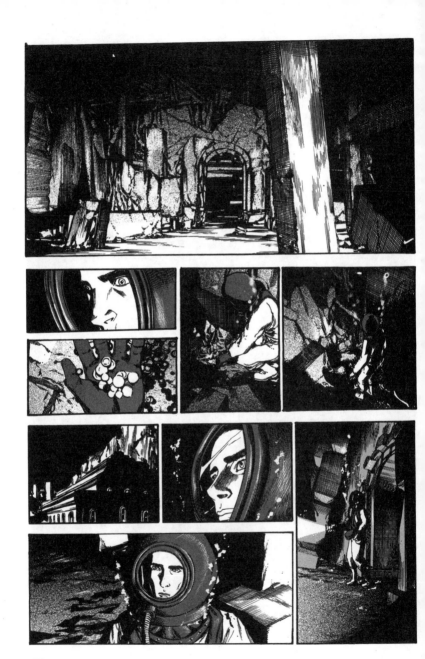

In time
what light
I had
weakened...

...and I
realized
I could
go no
further
into the
temple.

Someday this diary will be discovered. Follow where I could not, and reveal the mystery of a culture that was in its full noon of glory...

The artifacts are largely Hellenic in idea, of terrible antiquity... as though they were the remotest ancestor of Greek art.

...my last candle fades.

Alas...

...when cave dwellers roamed Europe, and the Nile flowed unwatched to the sea.

59

Light...?

Illusion... a trick of my mind.

Nonsense.

And I perceive the light... drifting in from the deep.

...I can reach out and touch it.

...the glass from which I last drank...

But I see...

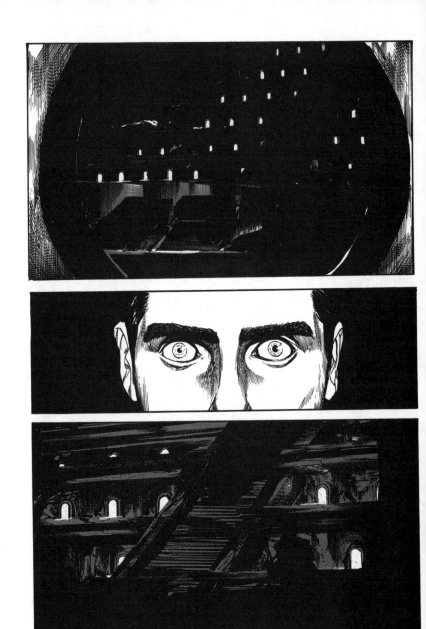

A rhythmic, melodic sound from the water...

Or...could it perhaps be the beam and beacon of a rescue ship...?

This, at least, must be illusion.

It cannot be real, so...

This delusion...

No.

...is of my own weakening mind.

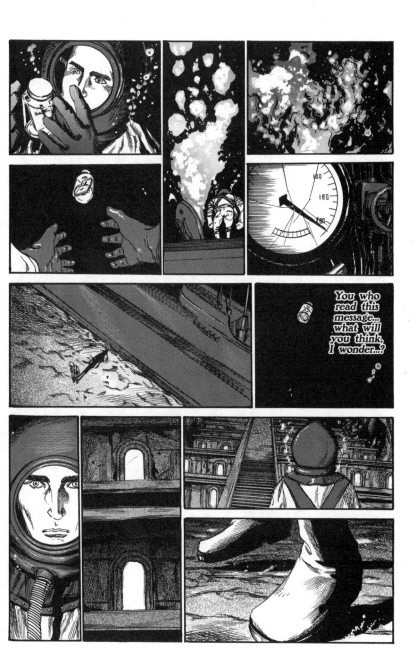

You who read this message... what will you think, I wonder...?

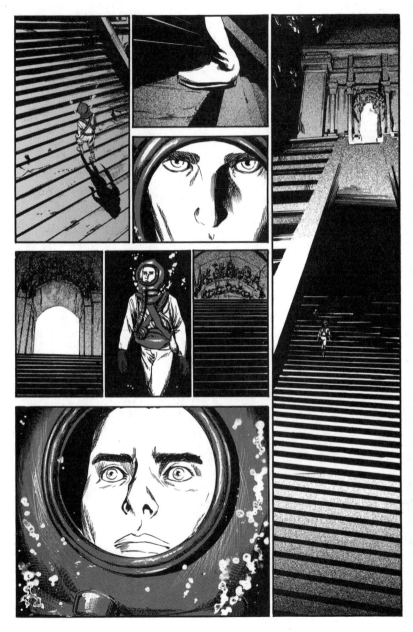

What I
am seeing
cannot
exist.

I have
gone
mad.

...to
enter
into that
primal
shrine...

Yet I
cannot
suppress
the urge...

...the silent secret of unfathomed waters and uncounted years.

魔犬

THE HOUND

H. P. LOVECRAFT'S
"THE HOUND"
Written in September 1922
Published in February 1924 in *Weird Tales*

May heaven forgive the folly and morbidity which led us both to so monstrous a fate.

God...

Esoteric studies... gruesome art. These things too became only diversions... only novelties.

SKFF

Romance... adventure... such commonplace joys soon grew stale.

My dear friend St. John and I... we had wearied of the ordinary world.

SKFF

SKFF

...and the diabolism of our penetrations. To things not of this earth...

We found the potency we sought only by increasing gradually the depth...

KLIK

CHAK

TAK

76

...but found below it.

CREAAAAAK

THUD

We craved the direct stimuli of unnatural personal experiences...

...in that hideous extremity of human outrage...

...the abhorred practice of grave robbing.

TOK

TOK

KLAK

TMP

COME
IN.

ST.
JOHN...
IT'S ME.

NOK

NOK

SOMETHING
TO EAT...?

I'M
FINE.

...NOT
SO WITH
YOU?

LINE
BY LINE,
I NEVER
TIRE
OF ITS
POETRY...

THE
NECRO-
NOMICON
...

ST.
JOHN...

BLUPP

I'VE ONLY READ IT TEN TIMES.

THMP

HEH.

...BUT IT IS SAID HIS ENGLISH VERSION IS... EXPURGATED.

THE MAGUS JOHN DEE TRANSLATED IT...

I LONG FOR A COPY OF THE ORIGINAL BOOK IN ARABIC BY ABDUL ALHAZRED...

ARE YOU READY TO DIG ONCE MORE...?

I HAVE LEARNED OF A CERTAIN MAN, FIVE CENTURIES LAID IN A HOLLAND CHURCHYARD.

IT SEEMS IN HIS TIME HE TOO WAS A GRAVE ROBBER--AND STOLE A POTENT THING FROM A MIGHTY SEPULCHER.

LET US DO IT UNDER THE FULL MOON.

I SEE... AND HAVE ONLY TO ASK...

WHEN?

...MY HEART POUNDS.

AN EXPEDITION... AFTER SO LONG AN ABSENCE...

KRNCH

KRNCH

KRNCH

HOWLLLLLL

CHEE
CHEE
CHEE

YES...

ONE THING I HAVE NOT TOLD YOU...

AROOOOOO

...THAT HIS CORPSE WAS FOUND TORN APART BY THE NAILS AND TEETH OF A GREAT BEAST.

...THE PEASANTS SAY OF THIS GRAVE ROBBER...

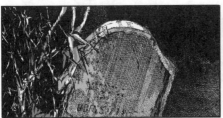

KRNCH

...

THE LIGHT...

KRNCH

TIME TO DIG.

THERE.

FWNCH

AND WHAT WONDERS AWAIT US...?

AAARROOOOO

...

ST. JOHN
...

...?!

ANOTHER DOG.

NO... SOME-THING ELSE...

GGRRRRRRR

WHOOOOOO

...PER-HAPS.

PERHAPS THE BEAST, COME BACK FOR OUR FINE GENTLEMAN.

HA, HA.

PRY IT OPEN.

THE COFFIN!

RUMMMMMBLE

KRRRCHH

500 YEARS DEAD...?

AMAZING...

HE'S HELD TOGETHER REMARKABLY WELL. YOU CAN STILL SEE THE MARKS OF THE BEAST.

AROUND HIS NECK... COULD IT BE...?

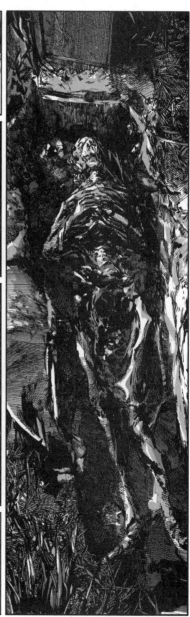

WHAT IS IT...?

LOOK.

AND THE INSCRIPTION...?

IT'S JADE...

...AN AMULET.

...THAT IN THIS SHAPE MANIFEST THOSE SOULS THAT VEXED AND GNAWED AT THE DEAD.

ABDUL ALHAZRED WRITES...

WORDS FROM THE *NECRONOMICON.* A WINGED HOUND... SOUL SYMBOL OF THE CORPSE-EATING CULT OF LENG.

WELL WORTH THE TRIP.

WONDERFUL.

WE FOUND TREASURE INDEED IN HOLLAND.

FWSSHHHHHH

WHERE SHALL WE DIG NEXT...?

ARooooooo...

THE HOWLING OF THE BEAST...

WHAT TROUBLES YOU?

...?

...DID YOU NOT HEAR IT?

...

OH, YES...

THE JEWEL OF OUR HOARD.

...MAGNIFI-CENT.

93

Eh...?

...A shadow passed.

COME IN, ST. JOHN...

NOK NOK NOK

EEE HEEE HEEE

CHAK

...

WHAT...

...WHAT IS IT?

UH...?

GET UP, ST. JOHN.

SOMEONE IS IN THE HOUSE.

...

A THIEF...

NO. THAT LAUGH WAS MEANT TO PROVOKE US.

NOT THE POLICE...

PLAYING WITH US...

SKRITCH SKRITCH

AN ENEMY.

BE WARNED... I SHOOT TO KILL.

CHAK

SKRITCH

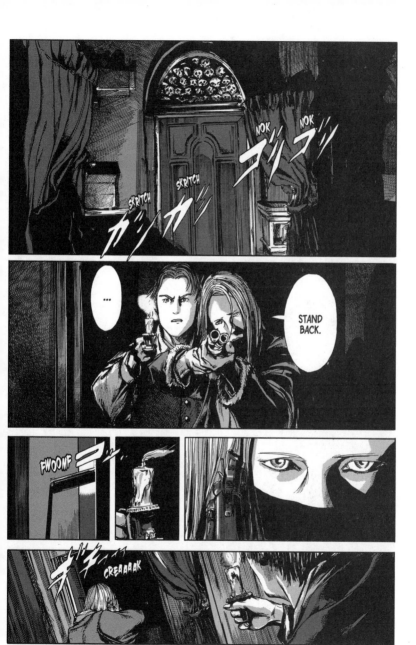

99

ST. JOHN... DID YOU HEAR THE VOICE...?

CHEE CHEEEE

BEYOND A DOUBT...

...IT WAS DUTCH... IT SPOKE OF THE ABYSS.

HOWLLLLLLL

...!

A BEAR...?

ST. JOHN! COME BACK INSIDE!!

...

NO, A DOG...

PLEASE, JOHN! INSIDE...

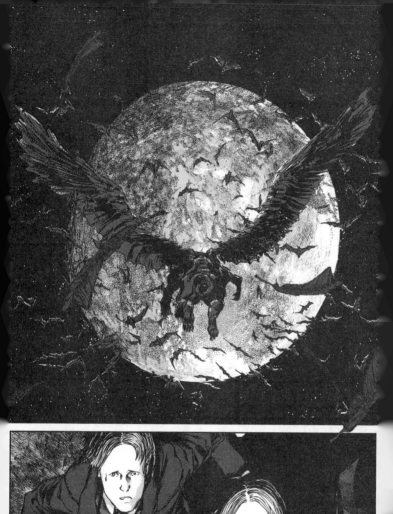

110

ST.
JOHN!!

AM...
ULET...

JOHN...

AM...

...AM...

...THAT...
DAMNED
THING...

ST.
JOHN!!

!!

...

HEH...

...!

MY APOLOGIES, BUT WE ARE CLOSING...

SIR...

...IT'LL FETCH A FAIR PRICE, DON'T YE THINK...?

AYE, LADS, THIS FINE BAUBLE...

...BUT STILL, I SHOULD PROFIT BY *THIS!*

HO, HO, HO! AYE, I'M UP TA NAE GOOD...

SEE...!

EH...?

KREEAK
KREEAK

...now snatched away like a wallet... by some common thief.

Compounding the horror was the sickly shame at the thought of the hideous treasure St. John and I had unearthed at such cost...

HULP! MOORD!

WAT GEBEURT ER?!

EEN AFSCHUWELIJKE DAAD...!

WHAT'S 'E SAYING...?

...FOUR MEN, TORN AND SAVAGED!

THE FOULEST CRIME IN MEMORY IN ROTTERDAM...

RUBBISH...

LIKE AN ANIMAL WAS AT 'EM...

...THAT'S THE NAME ON THE CASE.

HM...

YOUR PAPERS, SIR...?

OFFICER, THAT'S MINE...

...IT WAS STOLEN.

SOME- THING WRONG, SIR...?

...NO.

...

123

CAWWWW

125

126

SHIKK

HELL...

...

FWUMP

SHIKK

A dark mass writhed within the coffin.

....!

SHREEE

HOWWLLLLLLL

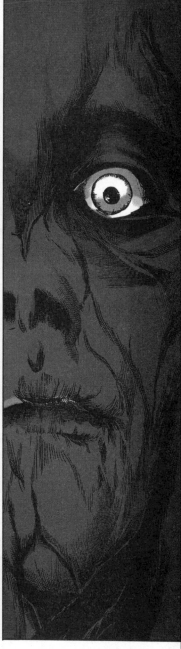

134

I heard the baying of the hound...

...the flapping of the wings closing around me.

And it was pointless to run any further.

BLAAMMMM

名もなき都

THE NAMELESS CITY

H. P. LOVECRAFT'S
"THE NAMELESS CITY"
Written in January 1921
Published in November 1921 in *The Wolverine*

As recorded in the Necronomicon, it was of this place that Abdul Alhazred the mad poet dreamed on the night before he sang his unexplainable couplet...

When I drew nigh the nameless city I knew it was accursed.

..."That is not dead which can eternal lie, // And with strange aeons even death may die."

ヒュゥゥゥ
WHHHHHHH

WHOOWHOOWHOO
ゴオォォ

WHOOOO

FWOOOOO

TAP

SHHHHK

...yet I was filled with dread to hear it.

Just the wind...

140

Untouched since it was abandoned.

Ancient before the first stones of Memphis were laid...while the bricks of Babylon were yet unbaked. There is no legend so old.

...this must be the city of myth.

At long last, I told myself...

A city never given a name. No hint remains of its past prosperity...

...all the tribes of Arabia shun it, without wholly knowing why.

Neither carving nor inscription remains outside to tell of those men, if men they were, who built the city.

Eh?

The night wind...

FWOOOOOO

When I came upon it in the ghastly stillness of unending sleep, it looked at me...

...chilly from the rays of a cold moon.

SHKK

And as I returned its look, I forgot my triumph at finding it.

WHOOOO

But I perceived that an hour would come when it would quiet...

FWOOOOOOO

The wind had not yet abated.

...and that the source of the wind was also the opening to what lay within.

CRACKLE

FWSHH

A buried altar, perhaps.

The ceiling was curiously low.

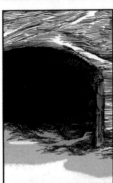

KLAK

And in the back...

147

It had been unmistakably a shrine for ceremonies.

No, this had been no dwelling space.

There came a gradual glow ahead.

...but these I was obliged to worm rather than walk.

A rough flight of many steeply descending stairs were carved out from the rock...

...it had in fact taken five hours.

The descent had seemed endless...

In the dim phosphorescence, I had not noticed that my torch had gone out.

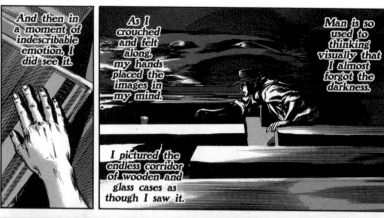

And then in a moment of indescribable emotion, I did see it.

As I crouched and felt along, my hands placed the images in my mind.

Man is so used to thinking visually that I almost forgot the darkness.

I pictured the endless corridor of wooden and glass cases as though I saw it.

150

They were no relics of crudity like the temples in the city above.

In their golden hue and exquisite clear lids, they were magnificent in their surfaces.

The cases were of polished wood, topped by thick glass...

...how did they linger for so long intact in this abysmal place...?

In their shapes, oblong and horizontal, they were hideously like coffins.

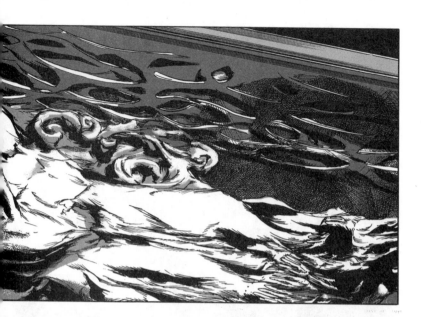

Most were gorgeously enrobed in the costliest of fabrics... laden with ornaments of gold, jewels, and unknown shining metals.

...but
there was
still more
to see.

They could
not have
been real.
Perhaps
elaborately
fashioned
idols, I
thought...

Some
palaeogean
species that
had lived
when the
nameless city
was alive.

...and the creatures that had built it!

...told the history of this place...

The frescoes on the walls and ceiling...

...of a society now lost, but once greater than Egypt and Chaldea.

A bizarre allegory, surely. These creatures were like the totems of Indian tribes, or the she-wolf of the ancient Romans. The people whose bare city remained above had once, in these depths, enshrined this grotesque foundation myth...

I was, however, mistaken that there were no humans depicted here.

This explained why no humans were depicted...

...for these shapes, these masks, stood for the men of that vanished civilization.

156

In the final image of all, their last priests, near death, still had the spite to hack and slay a band of primitive creatures... different from them.

As the fresco completed its slow spiral of ages, the creatures seemed to gradually waste away in body... though their spirit, shewn as a hovering form above the city ruins, waxed ever greater under the moon.

And I remembered how the Arabs fear the nameless city.

Small, numerous steps, like those of the black paths I had traversed.

Beyond the portal, in the radiance, I could see the head of a steep flight of steps.

158

Swung back open from the portal were massive doors of brass...

...thick enough to seal this uttermost light away from the vaults and passages above.

A uniform radiance... dazzling from a spreading sky.

After a
few feet,
the glow-
ing vapors
concealed
everything.

...and beneath
that sunlit
mist, it was
below that lay
the world.

Rather than
great depths,
it seemed
the peak
of Mount
Everest...

...nor
cloud...

But this
was
neither
mist...

...but hatred
and primal
hostility.

At last I understood...

...the nature of that shrieking, moaning wind...

...from the gulf of the inner earth.

It was their voices, coming forth and returning... keeping the nightly cycle of their age-long grudge.

165

KREEEEAK

...the men who were torn to pieces by the nameless race beneath the nameless city...who shall never cease resenting young humanity...the witless children who supplanted them in the weakness of their age.

In the ceasing of the night-winds I compared myself to the only other human image in that frightful corridor...

It is said that Abdul Alhazred was devoured by an invisible monster in 738 AD.

HAHH

In the clawing of the swirling currents there seemed to abide a vindictive rage all the stronger...

...because it was largely impotent.

THE END

H. P. LOVECRAFT'S
THE HOUND
and Other Stories

A sleepless night. A presence at the door. A whispering, barely heard. An anxiety and fear such as you haven't felt since you were young. An intuition of primordial death. Lovecraft was a writer who crafted such unknowable darkness—a priest of his own Mythos. I know fear even at the richness of his creativity.

By illustrating his stories, I intend to become an apostle of the gods he made. I do not feel my work is yet complete. The images swell in my mind. "If I draw it like this . . ." "If I do it this way . . ." I hear the divine voice, commanding me to continue.

I am blessed that you are reading this. You have my gratitude.

2014, High Summer
Gou Tanabe

ABOUT THIS BOOK AND THE ARTIST

田
辺
剛

Gou Tanabe is known in Japan for using the manga format to adapt literary works, including Maxim Gorky's "Twenty-Six Men and a Girl" and Anton Chekhov's "The House with the Mezzanine." The first Lovecraft story in this collection, "The Temple," was originally serialized in the March and April 2009 issues of Japan's acclaimed manga anthology magazine *Comic BEAM*, home of other works available in English such as Mari Yamazaki's *Thermae Romae*, Kaoru Mori's *Emma*, and Takako Shimura's *Wandering Son*. Readers familiar with twentieth-century history will note that Gou Tanabe's adaptation of "The Temple" moves it from its original World War I setting to World War II. The other two stories in this collection, "The Hound" and "The Nameless City," were published in the July and August 2014 online issues, respectively, of *Comic Walker*. Dark Horse hopes to publish further volumes of Tanabe's Lovecraft adaptations in the future.

President and Publisher
MIKE RICHARDSON

Designer
CINDY CACEREZ-SPRAGUE

Digital Art Technician
CHRISTINA McKENZIE

English-language version produced by Dark Horse Comics

Published by Dark Horse Manga
A division of Dark Horse Comics, Inc.
10956 SE Main Street
Milwaukie, OR 97222

DarkHorse.com

To find a comics shop in your area, call the Comic Shop Locator Service toll-free at 1-888-266-4226

First edition: July 2017
ISBN 978-1-50670-312-1

10 9 8 7 6 5 4 3 2 1
Printed in the United States of America

the KUROSAGI corpse delivery service

黒鷺死体宅配便

Five young students at a Buddhist university find there's little call for their job skills in today's Tokyo ... among the *living*, that is! But their studies give them a direct line to the dead—the dead who are still trapped in their corpses, and can't move on to the next reincarnation! Whether you died from suicide, murder, sickness, or madness, they'll carry your body anywhere it needs to go to free your soul! Written by Eiji Otsuka of the notorious *MPD-Psycho*!

Volume 1:
ISBN 978-1-59307-555-2 $10.99

Volume 2:
ISBN 978-1-59307-593-4 $10.99

Volume 3:
ISBN 978-1-59307-594-1 $10.99

Volume 4:
ISBN 978-1-59307-595-8 $10.99

Volume 5:
ISBN 978-1-59307-596-5 $10.99

Volume 6:
ISBN 978-1-59307-892-8 $10.99

Volume 7:
ISBN 978-1-59307-982-6 $10.99

Volume 8:
ISBN 978-1-59582-235-2 $10.99

Volume 9:
ISBN 978-1-59582-306-9 $10.99

Volume 10:
ISBN 978-1-59582-446-2 $10.99

Volume 11:
ISBN 978-1-59582-528-5 $11.99

Volume 12:
ISBN 978-1-59582-686-2 $11.99

Volume 13:
ISBN 978-1-61655-067-7 $12.99

Volume 14:
ISBN 978-1-61655-739-3 $12.99

THE KAZUO KOIKE LIBRARY FROM DARK HORSE MANGA

LONE WOLF AND CUB OMNIBUS
Volume 1:   ISBN 978-1-61655-134-6
Volume 2:   ISBN 978-1-61655-135-3
Volume 3:   ISBN 978-1-61655-200-8
Volume 4:   ISBN 978-1-61655-392-0
Volume 5:   ISBN 978-1-61655-393-7
Volume 6:   ISBN 978-1-61655-394-4
Volume 7:   ISBN 978-1-61655-569-6
Volume 8:   ISBN 978-1-61655-584-9
Volume 9:   ISBN 978-1-61655-585-6
Volume 10:   ISBN 978-1-61655-806-2
Volume 11:   ISBN 978-1-61655-807-9
Volume 12:   ISBN 978-1-61655-808-6
$19.99 each

NEW LONE WOLF AND CUB
Volume 1:   ISBN 978-1-59307-649-8
Volume 2:   ISBN 978-1-61655-357-9
Volume 3:   ISBN 978-1-61655-358-6
Volume 4:   ISBN 978-1-61655-359-3
Volume 5:   ISBN 978-1-61655-360-9
Volume 6:   ISBN 978-1-61655-361-6
Volume 7:   ISBN 978-1-61655-362-3
Volume 8:   ISBN 978-1-61655-363-0
Volume 9:   ISBN 978-1-61655-364-7
Volume 10:   ISBN 978-1-61655-365-4
Volume 11:   ISBN 978-1-61655-366-1
$13.99 each

SAMURAI EXECUTIONER OMNIBUS
Volume 1:   ISBN 978-1-61655-319-7
Volume 2:   ISBN 978-1-61655-320-3
Volume 3:   ISBN 978-1-61655-531-3
Volume 4:   ISBN 978-1-61655-567-2
$19.99 each

PATH OF THE ASSASSIN
Volume 1:   ISBN 978-1-59307-502-6
Volume 2:   ISBN 978-1-59307-503-3
Volume 3:   ISBN 978-1-59307-504-0
Volume 4:   ISBN 978-1-59307-505-7
Volume 5:   ISBN 978-1-59307-506-4
Volume 6:   ISBN 978-1-59307-507-1
Volume 7:   ISBN 978-1-59307-508-8
Volume 8:   ISBN 978-1-59307-509-5
Volume 9:   ISBN 978-1-59307-510-1
Volume 10: ISBN 978-1-59307-511-8
Volume 11:   ISBN 978-1-59307-512-5
Volume 12: ISBN 978-1-59307-513-2
Volume 13: ISBN 978-1-59307-514-9
Volume 14: ISBN 978-1-59307-515-6
Volume 15: ISBN 978-1-59307-516-3
$9.99 each

COLOR OF RAGE
ISBN 978-1-59307-900-0
$14.99

CRYING FREEMAN
Volume 1: ISBN 978-1-59307-478-4
Volume 2: ISBN 978-1-59307-488-3
Volume 3: ISBN 978-1-59307-489-0
Volume 4: ISBN 978-1-59307-498-2
Volume 5: ISBN 978-1-59307-499-9
$14.99 each

LADY SNOWBLOOD
Volume 1: ISBN 978-1-59307-385-5
Volume 2: ISBN 978-1-59307-443-2
Volume 3: ISBN 978-1-59307-458-6
Volume 4: ISBN 978-1-59307-532-3
$14.99 each

FOR MATURE READERS

DRIFTERS

KOHTA HIRANO

Heroes from Earth's history are deposited in an enchanted land where humans subjugate the nonhuman races. This wild, action-packed series features historical characters such as Joan of Arc, Hannibal, and Rasputin being used as chess pieces in a bloody, endless battle!

From Kohta Hirano, creator of the smash-hit *Hellsing*, *Drifters* is an all-out fantasy slugfest of epic proportion!

VOLUME ONE	**VOLUME TWO**	**VOLUME THREE**
978-1-59582-769-2	978-1-59582-933-7	978-1-61655-339-5

$13.99 each

DARK
HORSE
MANGA

**AVAILABLE AT YOUR LOCAL COMICS SHOP OR BOOKSTORE
TO FIND A COMICS SHOP IN YOUR AREA, CALL 1-888-266-4226**
For more information or to order direct: On the web: DarkHorse.com ·E-mail: mailorder@darkhorse.com
·Phone: 1-800-862-0052 Mon.–Fri. 9 AM to 5 PM Pacific Time.

Drifters © Kouta Hirano. Originally published in Japan in 2010 by Shonen Gahosha Co., Ltd., Tokyo. English translation rights arranged with Shonen Gahosha Co., Ltd., Tokyo through Tohan Corporation, Tokyo. (BL 7092)

HELLSING

VOLUME 1:
ISBN 978-1-59307-056-4

VOLUME 2:
ISBN 978-1-59307-057-1

VOLUME 3:
ISBN 978-1-59307-202-5

VOLUME 4:
ISBN 978-1-59307-259-9

VOLUME 5:
ISBN 978-1-59307-272-8

VOLUME 6:
ISBN 978-1-59307-302-2

VOLUME 7:
ISBN 978-1-59307-348-0

VOLUME 8:
ISBN 978-1-59307-780-8

VOLUME 9:
ISBN 978-1-59582-157-7

VOLUME 10:
ISBN 978-1-59582-498-1

$13.99 EACH

AVAILABLE AT YOUR LOCAL COMICS SHOP OR BOOKSTORE!
To find a comics shop in your area, call 1-888-266-4226.

For more information or to order direct visit DarkHorse.com or call 1-800-862-0052
Mon.-Fri. 9 AM to 5 PM Pacific Time. Prices and availability subject to change without notice.

DarkHorse.

CREEPY AND EERIE

PRESENTS PRESENTS

Bringing you the finest compilations of the
best-known names in horror comics!

BERNIE WRIGHTSON

ISBN 978-1-59582-809-5 $19.99

RICHARD CORBEN

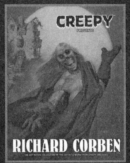

ISBN 978-1-59582-919-1 $29.99

STEVE DITKO

ISBN 978-1-61655-216-9 $19.99

ALEX TOTH

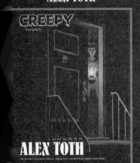

ISBN 978-1-61655-692-1 $19.99

EL CID

ISBN 978-1-61655-015-8 $15.99

HUNTER

ISBN 978-1-59582-810-1 $19.99

EERIE

A R C H I V E S

GET THEM NOW
$49.99 EACH

Volume
ISBN 978-1-59582-245-

Volume
ISBN 978-1-59582-315-

Volume
ISBN 978-1-59582-369-

Volume
ISBN 978-1-59582-525-

Volume
ISBN 978-1-59582-353-

Volume
ISBN 978-1-59582-569-

Volume
ISBN 978-1-59582-703-

Volume
ISBN 978-1-59582-760-

Volume
ISBN 978-1-59582-773-

Volume 1
ISBN 978-1-59582-719-

Volume 1
ISBN 978-1-59582-775-

Volume 1
ISBN 978-1-59582-996-

Volume 1
ISBN 978-1-61655-087-

Volume 1
ISBN 978-1-61655-159-

Volume 1
ISBN 978-1-61655-236-

Volume 1
ISBN 978-1-61655-400-

Volume 1
ISBN 978-1-61655-476-

Volume 1
ISBN 978-1-61655-520-

Volume 19
ISBN 978-1-61655-643-

Volume 2
ISBN 978-1-61655-850-

Volume 2
ISBN 978-1-61655-896-

Volume 2
ISBN 978-1-50670-006-

CHANT IN REVERSE

Gou Tanabe's manga adaptation of H. P. Lovecraft's stor
drawn in the traditional Japanese comics style, whose pc
panel order reads the opposite of the Western order, rig
left. Please turn the book around to begin reading.

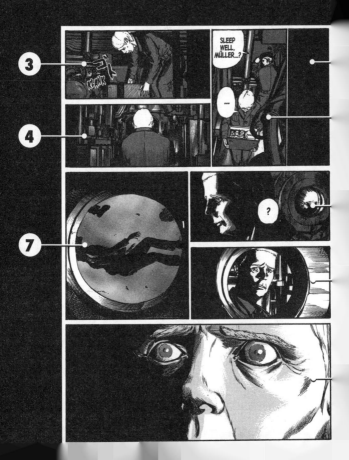